PRAISE THROUGH SUDDEN DEVASTATION

Millie Joy Radosti

All rights reserved. This book is protected by the copyright laws of the United States of America. No portion of this book may be stored electronically, transmitted, copied, reproduced, or reprinted for commercial gain or profit without prior written permission from the authors except as allowed per fair use guidelines. Only the use of short quotations for reviews or as reference material in other works and occasional page copying for personal or group study is allowed without written permission. Permission requests may be emailed to .

All Scripture quotations are taken from the Holy Bible, New Living Translation, copyright ©1996, 2004, 2015 by Tyndale House Foundation. Used by permission of Tyndale House Publishers, a Division of Tyndale House Ministries, Carol Stream, Illinois 60188. All rights reserved.

All Scripture quotations marked (AMP) are taken from the Amplified Bible, Copyright © 1954, 1958, 1962, 1964, 1965, 1987 by The Lockman Foundation. Used by permission. www.Lockman.org

All Scripture quotations marked (ESV) are from the ESV® Bible (The Holy Bible,

English Standard Version®), copyright © 2001 by Crossway, a publishing ministry of Good News Publishers. Used by permission. All rights reserved.

All Scripture quotations marked (KJV) are taken from the King James Version unless otherwise noted. Public domain.

All Scripture quotations marked (NIV) are taken from the Holy Bible, New International Version®, NIV®. Copyright © 1973, 1978, 1984, 2011 by Biblica, Inc.™ Used by permission of Zondervan. All rights reserved worldwide. www.zondervan.com The "NIV" and "New International Version" are trademarks registered in the United States Patent and Trademark Office by Biblica, Inc.™

All Scripture quotations marked (NKJV) are taken from the New King James Version®. Copyright © 1982 by Thomas Nelson. Used by permission. All rights reserved.

All Scripture quotations marked (TPT) are from The Passion Translation®. Copyright © 2017, 2018 by Passion & Fire Ministries, Inc. Used by permission. All rights reserved. www.thePassionTranslation.com.

TABLE OF CONTENTS

ENDORSEMENTS	1
INSIGHTS FROM THE EDITOR	9
FOREWORD	11
INTRODUCTION	15
CHAPTER 1: TRAUMA AND SPIRITUAL OBJECT PERMANENCE	25
CHAPTER 2: ACCOUNTIBILITY 101	41
CHAPTER 3: HEALTHY COMMUNITY	59
CHAPTER 4: LIVING ABOVE REPROACH	77
CHAPTER 5: TRANSFORMATION	107
CONCLUSION	225
RESOURCE PAGE	243

DEDICATED TO THOSE WHOSE FAITH WAS SHIPWRECKED AS A RESULT OF TRAUMA AND ABUSE. I SEE YOU. I CARE. YOU ARE HEARD. I BELIEVE YOU. LET'S BEGIN THE REST OF OUR LIVES!

A SPECIAL DEDICATION TO THE HONEST, HARDWORKING CHURCH LEADERS OF INTEGRITY:

Whether pastor, apostle, prophet, teacher or evangelist, I want to thank you for taking the time to pick up this book. This is a challenging yet needed topic. Although this useful tool can help you and those in your care navigate some of the most difficult matters, there are other considerations. The boundaries recommended in this book are designed to help those who have been through trauma and abuse so that these individuals can be validated in their experiences. Many times, when the standards of leadership are blurred for those who are traumatized, what has been done to them seems normalized. The traumatized need to hear someone, especially a leader, say, "What was done to you was wrong. I hear you. I believe you. This should have never happened to you. We must have incredibly high standards in the body of Christ. We will not endorse this level of abuse within our communities. You are safe to heal here."

At the same time, I address powerful topics, including false accusations and imperfections as human leaders. I am in ministry as well, and people have come into my home, family, and life with agendas birthed from their own brokenness. I've had people accuse and try to injure us. I'm not naive to the reality that ministers, especially those with integrity, go through immense seasons of pain and imperfections at times.

This book can be used as a resource to empower men and women of God who have dedicated their lives to his call but are left speechless and in shambles during the wake of exposure in a social media generation. We know how to educate and disciple people on forgiveness, but when it comes to true, devastating trauma and navigating community around the topic, we are completely lost as to what to say or do.

There is no perfect framework for a church nor is there a perfect leader outside of Jesus Christ himself. As a leader, if you are struggling or have made mistakes, there's grace for you. I encourage you to walk out the process of your healing as well. Boldly face the ways you have been hurt by the exposures of the church as a leader. These exposures deeply hurt everyone in a clergy position. I'm sorry for all you have been through, and I pray this resource is useful to you not only as a leader with others in your care but for you personally.

Additionally, let's raise the bar. Let's solidify the standard. If you are consistently burned out in ministry, incorporate a team around you to pray and navigate better boundaries and self-care so that you can finish the race you are called to in ministry. There will always be ministry-related stressors, but they can be navigated.

Check out my husband, Rob Radosti's, book *Happy Holiness*, for a sense of rejuvenation. And lastly, I want to thank you for your integrity and hard work. This book is not only about trauma and abuse for those who have endured but a celebration of healthy leaders who stand up for what is right and listen to those who have felt silenced in the wake of these issues. I want those who are suffering to find safety in *your* congregations, services, conferences, revivals, and events.

I look forward to all God will do in and through you and your ministries. This is the rebirth of making the church a safe place. This is one of the greatest revivals of the church to date. Thank you, leader, for your dedication to this call.

ENDORSEMENTS

Millie Joy Radosti writes this book not only from the perspectives gleaned from her personal devastating journey through brokenness, but also from valuable revelation and insights she gained during her pursuit of wholeness. With faith fully intact, she sought professional counsel on a number of levels, and also invested into a deep educational dive on the subjects of abuse, trauma, and mental illness. Millie Joy is one who has persevered in the midst of everything that attempted to come against her, and she has experienced ongoing freedom. As a result, she has a passion to see others walk free from the shackles that bind them so they can receive healing and wholeness.

I have observed Millie contend for freedom and understanding, and I have delighted in watching her always return to focus on Jesus, no matter what she faced. You will enjoy her genuineness, candor, faith, and valuable insights as you read Praise Through Sudden

Endorsements

Devastation. There is hope for the hopeless. There is freedom for the oppressed. There is help for the helpless. There is healing for the wounded. This is Millie's heart, conviction, and message.

Patricia King
Minister, Author, Media Host, and Producer
PatriciaKingMinistries.com

This book is a gift to the body of Christ from seasoned ministers who serve in a way that is both rare and priceless: They minister together as a family. And as a family, they have been vulnerable about their victories and struggles, which is part of what makes the Radostis so valuable and relevant. *Praise through Sudden Devastation* has obviously been born in the trenches. It isn't mere theory. It's practical wisdom that real people can apply in a real world. When it comes to dealing with opposition from dark forces, it's easy to partner with a spirit of fear. Because of that, leaders sometimes promote teachings that exploit that fear to generate a response.

But this book is a work of christological triumph. You will gain confidence in the finished work of the cross and be empowered to enforce by faith the victory of Jesus Christ once and for all. From generational curses to deliverance, you will discover that the cross actually worked, and you'll learn to engage with the enemy from a place of victory.

Bill & Traci Vanderbush
Authors/Speakers
BillVanderbush.com

Millie Radosti has written an incredibly important and timely book on triumphing over trauma! She skillfully guides us through the healing journey into the wholeness that God has called us to. Millie's own story of surviving and overcoming deep traumatic wounds from her childhood and church abuse empowers the powerful and life-changing truths she pours out in this amazing book. This book beautifully demonstrates the union of great biblical insight with psychological wisdom, expressing a deep understanding of

Endorsements

both topics. God is answering the cry of a hurting generation by giving us this book!

Dr. Michael Maiden
Sr. Pastor, Church for the Nations
Phoenix, Arizona
CFTN.com

To those who have suffered the trauma of abuse, Millie Radosti paints a bold picture of a new life beyond the pain: a scriptural response where the hurts and devastation of the past can be transformed by practical interventions and grounded wisdom to help you find hope and peace even after years of suffering. No matter your past, let Millie walk you through her story and those of others to give you direction and hope for a new life in Christ.

Fergus Scarfe
UK Regional Director, GOD.TV

Millie Joy Radosti is an incredible example of overcoming personal devastation, abuse, and trauma to walk in radical transformation. Her courageous journey into freedom and wholeness gives hope to every wounded person, hope that healing is available.

In her profoundly vulnerable and honest book *Praise Through Sudden Devastation*, Millie offers biblical wisdom, hard-fought insight, and practical steps into transformation to abused and hurting hearts. We have personally observed Millie and her husband, Rob, push past devastating circumstances and personal pain to pursue God's promise of freedom. This took grit, courage, and unwavering faith in God's goodness, no matter what. As you read, this same grit and courage will touch your heart and offer real hope partnered with wisdom forged in the fire.

Millie's story will be a faith catalyst to inspire your own story of healing and victory in Jesus. We are thankful for this timely book and the courageous journey that enabled Millie to live its powerful message.

Endorsements

Ben and Jodie Hughes
Pour It Out Ministries ~ PourItOut.org

Millie Radosti is an extraordinary example of a life that has been transformed and healed by divine love. This love, which is accessible to everyone, brings true freedom and deliverance and is found in Jesus Christ. In her book, *Praise Through Sudden Devastation*, Millie outlines a pathway for those who are hurting to find healing, for the abused to receive nurturing and care, and for the tormented to regain their joy and peace. Through her own personal journey, Millie offers an opportunity for individuals who have experienced abuse and trauma to break free from negative patterns and embrace a healthier way of living. Her story will inspire and deeply touch you as you witness her courage and perseverance. By reading her book, you will receive a powerful impartation for breakthrough, even in situations that may seem impossible.

Janet Mills, author, *Childbirth in the Glory*
JanetMills.com

We believe there are no accidents in life. The divine Creator has a plan for everything. We've come to the conclusion that everything boils down to the Scripture verses in 2 Corinthians 1:3–4. "Blessed be the God and Father of our Lord Jesus Christ, the Father of mercies and God of all comfort, who comforts us in all our tribulation, that we may be able to comfort those who are in any trouble, with the comfort with which we ourselves are comforted by God" (NKJV).

We've known this amazing mother, wife, and minister for many years. She continually amazes us with her determination and quest for truth and righteousness. Sometimes we have to be willing to bear our own soul in order to help others. That's exactly what Millie has done here. In life, many challenges will arise, both in churches and in the secular realm. Proven methods will help us navigate these issues and are essential to gain victory.

We consider Millie Joy to be an overcomer who has taken the trials and tragedies she has been through and has found sound solutions through the Word of God to help others conquer their darkest hours.

You may read this book and say, "How did she know this? That's exactly what happened to me." Don't stop reading until you've received your breakthrough. Jesus is waiting to bring freedom to you. Don't give up, and you just may find out that you, too, can comfort others with the comfort God himself has given you.
Thank you, Millie! May the Lord bless you for your hard work.

Pastors Mike and Debbie Sirianni
New Day Church
Colfax, North Carolina
NewDayChurchHP.org

INSIGHTS FROM THE EDITOR

Dear reader,

As Millie Joy's editor since 2017, I had the privilege of being one of the first to read her brand-new book, Praise through Sudden Devastation. Wow! Due to the nature of my business, I endorse only a tiny percentage of the books I edit. However, I am beyond honored to enthusiastically endorse this book.

While clergy abuse has been a problem in the church since the first century, instant access to the news and social media has brought with it an increasing awareness of this issue. Every day, more clergy members seem to be exposed, no matter the denomination: Catholic, Baptists, Methodists, charismatics, and more.

Nearly all of us have been impacted, whether personally or because family members or dear friends have been victims of abuse. How should we respond? What should we do now?

Insights from the Editor

Is there hope after the destructive effects of abuse and the resulting trauma?

Millie Joy's timely book, Praise through Sudden Devastation, was written to address this serious subject. Jam-packed with Scripture and with practical advice, Millie navigates this difficult topic with finesse and grace. Pulling on her degree in counseling and her graduate studies in social work, Millie skillfully weaves together best practices in the mental health field, biblical principles, and faith in the power of our healing and loving Father. She shows how these are not contradictory but complement each other, working to bring healing to those who have suffered at the hands of predators.

If you are looking for a no-nonsense yet grace-filled approach to abuse, trauma, and healing in the church, grab your copy of this powerful and life-changing book today! You'll be glad you did.

Happy reading,
Lisa Thompson
Professional Editor

FOREWORD

Very few people go looking for pain. We are not wired to experience abuse on any level. We are created to be loved, valued, accepted, and live within a healthy community. However, many people find themselves caught in the wake of someone else's storm. Within that storm, they experience trauma and abuse. While this is confusing in any situation, it is incredibly confusing when it happens within the church body. Or, as Millie states, "Wherever there are people, there is a potential for misunderstanding, lies, pain, and betrayal, and the list goes on."

Over the past number of years, we have seen an increasing number of high-profile pastors and leaders accused of various levels of spiritual and sexual abuse. Within the wake of this, we have even more people who have experienced this abuse within the church and are trying to put their lives back together.

Foreword

Some have left the church but still love the Lord; some have left the Lord, as the very one sent to shepherd the flock abused the sheep. Others are being a voice in this vast wilderness and providing a pathway to freedom.

Millie is standing firm and saying that God has a way of healing and freedom. As she faces the reality of sin and abuse within the church, she will invite you to come face-to-face with the only one who brings true healing, empowers forgiveness, and binds up your wounded heart. You will discover that you don't have to be defined by your experience. There is help, and there is more to life. You don't need to run away from the Lord, but you can run to Him, even in the confusion
and the pain.

However, Millie also goes beyond the pain we may encounter within the church to the pain we encounter in the world. While not denying the struggle, questions, emotions, and feelings, Millie shares how God ultimately has the victory. In any area of our lives, he does not cause abuse or trauma, but He refuses to allow it to have the last say in our lives if we walk with Him and will allow Him to bring healing. I invite you to join Millie on this journey. However, don't read this book just for information.

Just as your pain and trauma were an interruption in your life, allow this book to be an intentional interruption in your life. Read it slowly and take time to read all the Scriptures and journal your thoughts. Allow yourself to feel the emotions and take them to the Lord. Allow the Holy Spirit to take Heaven-formulated lens cleaner to your lenses and learn to see life differently. No matter what you have experienced, you are not damaged goods but a beloved son or daughter of the Most High God. Now, grab that cup of coffee, Bible, and journal. Find a comfortable chair and get ready to grow in the Lord and find freedom and healing that only comes from Him. It is worth the time and the journey!

Blessings,
Rev. Ruth Hendrickson

Touched by Jesus Ministry, Inc
DBA RHM International

Mashah Ministry
Mashahministry.com
RuthHendrickson.com

INTRODUCTION

The Church community is no stranger to trauma and abuse. One of the top controversies and criticisms has to do with church abuse scandals that leave devastation in their wake. Often the stage is set as follows: A long-time leader is surrounded by a church community. One day, seemingly out of nowhere, an allegation (or more than one) of abuse surfaces. Conflicted and loyal, the congregation pushes back against this reality, denying that the story could even be true.

But before it can be glossed over, more and more stories start coming to the surface. Confusion ensues, and the media starts to take the information and benefit from the dramatic ratings. What was once a sensitive and confusing situation is now the five o'clock news. The Church scrambles to do damage

Introduction

control. Accusations of gossip and insecurity make the rounds. Different groups with various motives advocate for investigations in and out of the church. All this movement. All this commotion. And countless people from the victims of the abuse to those who served so loyally and were impacted so deeply are forever changed.

In this tense time, people tend to run for cover. The victims learn quickly that they are seldom if ever believed, and if someone does seem to support them, it's hard to escape the skepticism and shame. Those who cling to loyalty may conflict with preset ideas of defending their leaders. Those who already had church trauma from other experiences may struggle to believe there is any hope for safety in the Church and conclude they may never be able to return.

This is not to bash Church or say there is no hope, but where there is imbalance, we must address the concerns. The generations that have emerged from Church trauma struggle to believe that Church is nothing more than a money-hungry business empire run on western theological ideas of consumerism and exploitation.

If you have been impacted by the reality of what I'm discussing here, this book is for you. However, this book doesn't only address church trauma; it encompasses various traumatic experiences and how we might grow so that we can build trust in our relationship with God, our relationships in the context of community and our relationship with ourselves.

We will discuss concepts that help us understand the reality of the presence of God despite our circumstances. We will come to a better understanding of what trauma and healing are. We will also discuss in great detail and gain clarity on the importance of accountability. When we've been hurt by those who have not been accountable and kept abuses covert, it can be very difficult to come to a place where we understand the need or desire for future accountability in our future.

We mustn't let our pain rob us of whole-person healing. In that, I encourage you to dive into topics that may scare you in this book. Don't avoid them. We need to look through the ugliness of the mindsets we've developed in order to see the beauty that these concepts carry. Concepts like accountability are only ugly when perverted and abused. They are designed to be a beautiful tool to help us remain healthy.

We will also discuss how true accountability can only be found in safe churches. But what does that look like? We need to address community specifically in the context of family as well. Many people have had a negative framework of what a family should look like because not everyone has come from a healthy family. Some have come from sick and disordered families or addicted families. We must gain insight on what a healthy family is in order to model healthy communities.

Other key points in this book include living above reproach, transformation in our lives, understanding our basic human needs, addressing trust, discerning how trauma affects our relationships and the resulting lenses we carry, differentiating between withdrawal and isolation, and considering the power of praise, especially in devastating times.

This book is not meant to be read like other books on this topic. This is because trauma is not something that can be described or understood by anything in the so-called normal world. Trauma is not normal. Trauma is another reality, another planet. When you go through trauma, you start to look at earth as if from a distance, as if you were standing on another planet. You may be yelling and screaming for people to see your pain and feel like you're light years away. When you try to talk about it, it's as if you are speaking in a strong dialect or language you don't understand. Going through trauma is like an alien experience.

With that said, this book will not be written in some self-help form from an educated expert on the subject who maintains a level of distance and superiority. (Don't you get enough of that in the help system?) I chose to go into my graduate program because I was a client first. The foundation of my experience is my personal experience before I went to academia. I've had amazing therapists and some pretty terrible ones. I've seen people in the field empathize and relate deeply. I've also seen the opposite. Regardless, I validate whatever perspective you have on therapy and getting help. I know the reality of it.

Since faith molds people's perspectives they have a variety of views about this. Some are anti-therapy, thinking it's all Freud-based and demonic. (It's not, but some in the field might lean this way. Therapy is like ministry in the sense that there can be a world of difference from church to church. The same is true from office to office when it comes to each individual or group therapy.) I will share my perspective.

Here is some of my experience:

If you've read my first book and some of my second, I share a lot of personal experience in this field from receiving therapy. I grew up in a ton of dysfunction and abuse. So much of it was normalized to me that I didn't know just how abnormal it was. I'm not saying hard circumstances and struggle in family systems is uncommon, just that it's not normal and healthy for brain development. Sometimes we have the tendency to think because things are common that they are normal. Then we tell ourselves we have no right to feel the way that we do. Of course, these thoughts don't connect rationally. We've been trained to make sense of what doesn't make sense since we were told that our emotions are dramatic and attention-seeking. Why have empathy for ourselves when it's not deemed productive by society? Where has all the empathy in society gone? And we wonder why narcissism is such an epidemic in our society.

So we get ourselves to the point where we find vices to help soothe those strong emotions that we don't know where they come from and don't have time to deal with. They aren't appropriate or controllable except perhaps with this substance or behavior. We just need that dopamine rush to self soothe. Maybe our parent passed away years ago, and we cannot even fathom to think about, much less cope with, that loss. It's in the distant past. Or maybe we are reminded of the divorce every time we try to establish family traditions with our children and our current spouse (if we have even managed to hope for another faithful significant other). Maybe we still get flashbacks from that assault, and we blame our puffy red eyes from crying in the bathroom on allergies to avoid undue questioning.

See, trauma doesn't mildly impact your life. It's like when you learn to manipulate Playdough as a child. You see how moldable it is. You can shape it how you like, but it doesn't decrease in volume. The same is true with trauma. Despite the coping method you chose, it doesn't go away. It just changes shape. So one day, you're broken from your divorce, and then you seem okay, but you just drink every night. You don't have a problem, but you also have an underlying anxiety of the thought of not having it.

Your social life changes to surround yourself with people who accept this lifestyle, and you start to see people who don't know how to loosen up with alcohol as too boring. Really, you have now developed a dependency, and you're already in a danger zone. From there, you start developing physical symptoms of addiction—trouble sleeping, migraines, and more—but if you stop your routine, your anxiety will push your depression into oblivion. "I think I need help." But you push this thought aside to try to get up for work the next day.

At work, you overhear your coworkers gossiping about the coworker who called out that day. "He's a complete drunk. He's on the verge of losing his kid." "Oh wow, I knew something was off about him. Poor kid. I know why his wife left him now."

At that point, you seriously realize that reaching out for help is not an option. Personal struggle equates to gossip and reputational damage. So the cycle continues.

Right?

Wrong!

If you relate to this story, I'm going to include some resources at the end of the book. Please flip there now to check them out.

Introduction

Alcohol is one example and there are tons of others. When I travel, I like to speak about my issue with self-injury in my younger years. In my early years in ministry, people sometimes wanted healing from their past so that scars were no longer visible. But I asked the Lord if I could keep mine. I even got a tattoo on them: the word *agape* in Greek because the unconditional love of God is the only thing in the world that could cover that level of pain and self-hatred.

Now I personally believe that therapy, inner healing, deliverance, and reaching out for help is so stigmatized because society has a way of denying what it needs. It's easier to demonize something that makes us vulnerable than to come to the reality that our walls are built to self-protect. We feel the risk is too great to tear the walls down and receive from the place of "I trust you with this broken part of me." It's much easier to develop an ego that infantilizes vulnerability.

CHAPTER ONE
TRAUMA AND SPIRITUAL OBJECT PERMANENCE

People often ask me how the Lord has brought me through all that He did. I can confidently say He has used therapy and even medications in my life. At times when I was weak, He provided resources to strengthen me. Sometimes those resources were a friend. Sometimes it was inner healing. Sometimes it was intensive therapy. Sometimes it was medications. Sometimes it was a church service. Whatever the case, He has never left me in my brokenness. And He won't leave you either. Scripture talks about this. "For God has said, 'I will never fail you. I will never abandon you'" (1 Thessalonians 13:5).

People will interpret this in different ways. When I started to feel the tangible presence of the Lord, I began to rely on it. But this verse was hard for me to interpret. If I didn't physically feel him, how could he be with me?

This concept is defined as spiritual object permanence. Object permanence is a concept developed by a founding father in the psychology field Jean Piaget, a child psychologist. An item exists, no matter what. But a developing child cannot understand this because they can't see or hear the item.[1]

Small children aren't born with object permanence. They call the first few months after birth the "fourth trimester" because babies aren't even aware that they are not still physically attached to their mother. As a mother myself, I have seen this concept in action. Everyone parents differently, but I chose to breastfeed on demand, so whenever my babies were hungry, I fed them. I wasn't strict on schedules but more attentive to their needs and natural body rhythms.

---

[1] Kendall K. Morgan, "Object Permanence: How Do Babies Learn It?," Web MD, November 21, 2023,
https://www.webmd.com/baby/what-age-do-babies-have-object-permanence.

For the first few months, the baby doesn't even always know whether it's day or night, especially when it comes to hunger. They don't understand, "It's one thirty a.m. and not two a.m. It's not time to eat yet, so I'll wait a half hour to cry even though I'm hungry." Nope. The baby lying in its bassinet feels hunger and screams for Mom. If Mom doesn't come, the baby's system kicks into survival. Now this is not against those who choose scheduled feedings. The baby does adjust to schedules for those who choose that, and pediatricians are great resources at helping guide parents here. I'm simply using my experience for the main point.

Before the baby adjusts to schedules (for the schedulers) or as the parents are learning the baby's natural body rhythms, each baby goes through at least some small spurts of time when they feel the hunger pang, and there is no food in that exact moment. They then turn to excessive crying to get the assistance they need in survival instinct.

We can be like this with God even as adults. Many suffer with spiritual object permanence.

Trauma and Spiritual Object Permanence

Some rely on some specific measure by which God has to reveal himself to them. They pray for an angelic encounter or some sign for God to prove he cares and is with them. But sometimes God doesn't. Did I say he doesn't show up? No. I say He shows up in the way we need, not always in the way we are demanding. Sometimes we are praying for a sign, and he sends us a phone call from a friend. Sometimes we're praying for an angelic encounter, and he sends us a sermon on our For You feed on TikTok. While it might sound silly, I fully believe God works in these ways.

Dare I say that sometimes God shows up by connecting us with therapeutic resources and medications? Well, I'm telling you just that. And these journeys are so individual, so I'm not saying anyone should live off any of these things from TikTok sermons to medications. I am saying God is *always* with you, and how he shows up can be different every single time.

Just because God hasn't shown up in ways that you were expecting, doesn't mean he's not present, aware, and responsive. He absolutely is.

DEVELOP YOUR SPIRITUAL OBJECT PERMANENCE

Look for ways God is providing healing resources. Did you quit therapy prematurely? Is he calling you to the prayer closet, and you've neglected that real personal undistracted prayer time for a while now?
In what ways can you see that God has been trying to reach you?

_____
_____
_____
_____
_____
_____
_____
_____
_____
_____
_____
_____
_____
_____
_____

TRAUMA

Trauma is defined as an injury, wound, psychiatric, or a behavior state that is disordered enough to cause ongoing illness.[2] A few years ago, the Lord gave me a deeper illustration of the term *trauma*.

One day, everything is normal. Reality is as such: The sun is shining. The birds are singing. You get into your car to head to work as usual. This isn't bad, though, because you love your job. You work in the career of your dreams. You're having lunch with a coworker today and picking up your kids for family movie night later. Everything thing is great. I wonder how the fam will like that stew simmering in the crock—*Bang!*

You didn't make it to work. In an instant, everything changed.

---

[2] Merriam-Webster Dictionary, s.v. "trauma (n.)," accessed January 3, 2024, https://www.merriam-webster.com/dictionary/trauma.

Hours later, you wake up in the hospital. You are informed that you were in an accident, and you've been unconscious. Your family surrounds you, and your daughter's face is soaked with tears. "Mom, I thought we lost you!" She wraps her arms around you.

You can hardly process the event; in fact, you only fully know what you are told. The hospital stabilizes you, and as the day progresses, you process with the care team and your family. Eventually, night falls, and the nurses try to make you comfortable for bed. As you drift off to sleep, you dream about the car scene that was once your reality. You're driving along, thinking about your plans for the day, as a car comes directly at your side of the vehicle. *Bang*! You wake up yelling and sweating, from flat to completely upright. Your heart is racing and you rapidly scan the room to try to figure out where you are. You're not in the car anymore; you realize you are still safe in your hospital bed, receiving treatment and recovering.

You're not in that car anymore, but somehow, your brain still is, and it's sending all the survival signals to the rest of your body. It's like you're stuck in the events of the crash over and over. It's like your entire brain has been interrupted.

TRAUMA IS AN INTERRUPTION

That's what trauma is: an interruption. When trauma enters your life, it interrupts everything that was once normal. It redefines it and changes your brain responses to what reality is for you.

One day, everything is one way, then the trauma interrupts everything. Until the interruption is addressed, nothing is ever the same again. I said in the beginning of this book that trauma is like living on another planet, looking down on planet earth. You recognize the interactions and the language, but you do not reciprocate. It's a new way of doing life. It's not comfortable, and in fact, once trauma hits, it can have the tendency to make a lot of other things worse.

One of my favorite Scriptures regarding

trauma follows: "Do not be conformed to this world, but be transformed by the renewal of your mind, that by testing you may discern what is the will of God, what is good and acceptable and perfect" (Romans 12:2 ESV).

This verse includes several key components starting with the words *conformed*, *transformed*, and *renewal*. I'll break those down shortly, but first take notice of the second part of the verse: "That by testing you may discern what is the will of God, what is good and acceptable and perfect." Trauma affects our discernment, our ability to understand the will of God, our knowledge of what is good and acceptable and even perfect.

The saying goes, "Hurt people hurt people." You can see this here in Romans. The verse directly talks about our ability to discern and even understand good after we've come to this fork in the road.

THE FORK IN THE ROAD

Trauma, the interruption, is a fork in the road.

Trauma and Spiritual Object Permanence

Picture yourself standing with a road leading to your left and a road leading to your right. One road is named Conformity, and the other is named Transformation. As painful as trauma can be, we actually have a choice. Sometimes, this takes a while to realize when we are at that fork in the road. One of the ways we can recognize this is when we are responding to life differently after we've been through a significant event. Maybe, like with my example, it's a car accident, but it might be an assault or rape or military service or processing a dysfunctional childhood in therapy. In that moment, you realize that life looks different, and what you used to handle, you don't even feel capable of handling anymore.

The fork in the road becomes more recognizable after the first few times you try to process life and even your day normally, but nothing is as it was before. Back home, after the car crash, you've been visited by countless friends and family. You've received therapies, and you're becoming physically stronger. Your church has prayed for you both in person and over their live-streamed service. Life is starting to seem close to reentry into normalcy.

The moment finally comes. The family wakes up. It's the day you are ready to get in your new car to head back to work. Just as you reach for the door handle, your heart starts racing. The blood in your body rushes to your head, and your breathing increases so much, you almost lose your breath. All at once the world starts spinning. Something is not right. Life is different now. What is going on? "I don't think I can do this." You shuffle your keys back in your purse, head into the house, collapse on the couch, and cry yourself to sleep.

Your life is officially interrupted at this point. Everything you once knew is different now. The crash has come and gone. You've been supported, and now you're supposed to be ready to venture back into life. Only you aren't.

Well-meaning people encourage you the best they can.

- It's over now. You just have to try.

Trauma and Spiritual Object Permanence

- Wasn't that accident six months ago?
- Aren't you better yet?

Nobody seems to truly understand that what you are feeling is beyond emotional. What you are feeling, you are feeling it everywhere in your physical body. Your brain is sending signals to the rest of your body as if you are being struck in that car crash over and over again.

At this point, most people start to recognize they need help but sometimes don't know where to turn. People start to consciously or subconsciously look for ways to soothe the panic that accompanies their trauma. Once the trauma has taken root, other factors also come into play. Shame starts to set in because you missed your first day back to work. Regret sets in because you've already lost six months of your life. Worry sets in as you're not the wife and mother you feel you should be, and it's not looking like it will get any better if you can't drive. Life is interrupted, and you're not sure if it will ever be the same again. On top of the pain and devastation, you are now carrying emotions like shame, regret, and fear.

This is the fork in the road.

CONFORMITY

Conforming to the patterns of the world is the road to maladaptive coping mechanisms. This includes addictions of all kinds and habits that rip you apart piece by piece. The fork in the road is an invitation to this path that offers temporary pseudo-numbing and counterproductive functionality.

The Greek word for *conformity* in this Scripture is συσχηματίζεσθε (pronounced: syschēmatizesthe). As you can see, in this verse, it means "to conform to" but breaking down the definition it actually even means "to identify with, take on the outward shape (externally), taking on similar outward form or expression, following the same pattern or being molded by."[3]

---

[3] Strong's Concordance, "4964. Suschématizó," Bible Hub, accessed January 3, 2024,
https://biblehub.com/greek/4964.htm.

When we come to the fork in the road, the road to conformity can look dangerously comfortable: alcohol, pills, old addictions or habits, wild sexual behavior and more. It may all start to look soothing, especially if you have a history with it. Take sexual behaviors, for example, which are so shamed by society and for good reason. Certain sexual behaviors can be dangerous, so society uses disapproval to try to prevent such behaviors.

But the person who engages in wild sexual behaviors can only be seen as the adult woman who dresses provocatively to engage with others in a way that supplies enough dopamine to soothe her pain because when she looks behind her, she sees that fork in the road. The road she chose looked like the best at the time because she recognized it. See, she was molested over and over again as a young girl. So she knew that if she engaged in wild sexual behaviors, she wouldn't experience rejection, at least in that moment. She knew she could engage her need for connection and merge it with the ways people would come close to her in the past.

The only issue is, she's not a little girl anymore. She's a woman, and those around her perceive her as such. She's expected to maintain stable relationships and provide food for her family. Instead, she's stumbling in from bars at two in the morning with smeared makeup. She's shamed because she should know better. And does she? Perhaps. And perhaps she's now at the point that these selfish actions feed her survival, at least for the moment, and well, she brushes the consequences off to that no one cares anyway.

She doesn't quite make the connection, but she's chosen conformity. She externally exhibits all the behaviors of the world even though, in her heart, she claims to maintain faith. She justifies her behaviors because her beliefs are rooted in a mixture of "nobody's perfect" along with lies she's accepted to make sense of her internalized pain.

There is good news, though. See, no matter how far down the road of conformity you travel, there's always a bridge. The bridge is this: "I need help." Now we can't cross the bridge over to the other side in one step. The bridge takes several steps to cross. Recognizing that you need help is only step one. Step two is talking about your need for help with someone who will hold you accountable.

CHAPTER TWO
ACCOUNTABILITY 101

Many struggle to define true accountability. Accountability is not simply someone who you associate with or who claims to know you. It's so much deeper than that. In this chapter, we will discuss how essential accountability is to us as believers in the Bible. "Therefore confess your sins to each other and pray for each other so that you may be healed. The prayer of a righteous person is powerful and effective" (James 5:16 NIV).

Confession is a powerful tool. Confession means to make a formal declaration of the sin you partake in, carry, or have done. Sometimes people get confused and think confession means accepting guilt and shame, but it's actually admitting it to set ourselves free.

Sometimes we dramatize what this will be like, but when we know that we have safe places to be accountable, we can see confession for what it is. It's a setting free. If you've never confessed your sins to a safe person, you are missing out. You'll notice that within a healthy community, confession is a beautiful and healing experience.

Of course, notice it doesn't stop there. Always finish off the confession to each other with prayer. Let your confession become your revival. It is powerful and effective, just as it says in God's Word.

"As iron sharpens iron, so one person sharpens another" (Proverbs 27:17 NIV). Iron is a very symbolic substance in the Bible. It can represent "affliction, chastisement (Deuteronomy 4:20; Ezekiel 22:18-22), barrenness (Deuteronomy 28:23), slavery (Deuteronomy 28:48), strength (Job 40:18), severity (Psalm 2:9), captivity (Psalms 107:10), and more. Figuratively, a yoke of iron (Deuteronomy 28:48) denotes hard service; a rod of iron (Psalms 2:9), a stern government; a pillar of iron (Jeremiah 1:18), a strong support; a furnace of iron (Deuteronomy 4:20), severe labour; a bar of iron (Job 40:18), strength; fetters of iron (Psalms

107:10), affliction; giving silver for iron (Isaiah 60:17), prosperity."[4]

In the context of Proverbs 27:17, Scripture tells us that other people make us better. At times, people (especially in abusive communities) will take the Bible out of context. Some interpret this to mean that we should make life harder on each other because they claim that iron reflects hardship, but this is not what it means.

I saw this in action one time when someone was promoting an atmosphere of competition among his leadership and staff. (This leader was extremely abusive, which would later be revealed to us.) Needless to say, I feel it's important to mention that the emphasis in this passage is on how good iron is for the other in their sharpening.

---

[4] Easton's Bible Dictionary, s.v. "iron (n.)," Bible Study Tools, accessed January 3, 2024, https://www.biblestudytools.com/dictionary/iron/#.

There are benefits to enduring the flames that together, and when we do it together, we become sharp together.

"So then, each of us will give an account of ourselves to God" (Romans 14:12 NIV). We are first and foremost accountable to God. Living accountable within our relationships here on earth prepares us for the moment we will give account of ourselves to God Himself. This will be a beautiful moment for us. Imagine being healed, having already confessed sin one to another, encouraging and praying for each other, and then approaching God with that very confidence and love. This is a beautiful thing, friends.

"Brothers and sisters, if someone is caught in a sin, you who live by the Spirit should restore that person gently. But watch yourselves, or you also may be tempted. Carry each other's burdens, and in this way you will fulfill the law of Christ" (Galatians 6:1–2 NIV). We already know that sin is healed through confession and prayer because Jesus took every sin on the cross for us already. A misconception with this passage is that a person in sin needs to be restored to their former position. Restoration starts with the internal security of the person themselves. The goal is not to restore abusive ministers to ministry. Many abusive ministers should never return to ministry, ever. The restoration begins within the person and their identity, then also how the sin has affected their family and community. The role the person plays in ministry is not the concern here. There is a way to go about that as well, but it may be another topic for another time.

In the restoration phase, when we are the ones gently restoring another, we must be careful of our judgements. We may think we are above certain sins or lifestyles, but the truth is, any of us can be deceived the moment we aren't aware of the possibility of deception. This kind of judgement opens the door to just that. So be restored and restore gently and judgement free!

"And let us consider how we may spur one another on toward love and good deeds, not giving up meeting together, as some are in the habit of doing, but encouraging one another—

and all the more as you see the Day approaching" (Hebrews 10:24–25 NIV). Amazingly, accountability isn't all confession and negativity. Accountability is exciting. Through accountability, we encourage each other, and our words and actions affect one another. We are expected to work on our awareness of how we impact those around us. We must work toward leaving a positive impact on others as we urge them to act in loving ways and complete good deeds. We must encourage coming together and encouraging each other. These are foundational principles but can also be challenging, especially when coming from a mindset of following a road of conformity. Nevertheless, we must journey on this step our entire lives!

"Plans fail for lack of counsel, but with many advisers they succeed" (Proverbs 15:22 NIV). I love how God's Word here doesn't mince words in the use of the word *advisor* but claims we need many advisors. I hope you are getting a picture of true community because this is a key part of it. We can be partial to those who we know will agree with us, but we must be open to much advice, even those God put in our lives who don't give us the answers we want to hear.

"And do not forget to do good and to share with others, for with such sacrifices God is pleased. Have confidence in your leaders and submit to their authority, because they keep watch over you as those who must give an account. Do this so that their work will be a joy, not a burden, for that would be of no benefit to you" (Hebrews 13:16–17 NIV). These sacrifices are not to be confused with the sacrifice Jesus made on the cross for our sins. They are the acknowledgement of the work and commitment needed to maintain a focus on what is good. This isn't some ritualistic competition for the completion of your sins. We know we can get into heaven because of Jesus's sacrifice. At the same time, while here on earth, we need to be doing good, serving, and sharing.

An important consideration is that we also need leaders who can handle their authority by living above reproach. When they live in a way that is accountable and safe, they have good fruit; then, yes, submitting to their authority can be a beautiful process. In return, they look after you too.

"Submit to one another out of reverence for Christ" (Ephesians 5:21 NIV). You will see this verse used in reference to marriage when people talk about the overall submission process, but it's not limited to marriage. (And of course, marriage is the utmost accountability.) But submission one to another works to establish that accountability doesn't have to be an unhealthy lordship of authority. There's room for communication and growth within an accountable relationship.

This term *submission* is used like a military term to "put oneself under" or "humble yourself."[5] The Bible later describes how we submit in marriage in ways that meet our spouse's needs, but that's slightly off topic for the context I'm addressing.

---

[5] "Lesson 3: What Do You Mean, 'Submit'? (Ephesians 5:21-24)," Bible.org, accessed January 3, 2024, https://bible.org/seriespage/lesson-3-what-do-you-mean-submit-ephesians-521-24.

The "submit ourselves one to another" alludes to a peer relationship on many levels. This is why many in the church are hurt when they pledge accountability to a leader over them who does not live this out within the context of community themselves. A leader who will extract information about you and then maintain the appearance of perfection is a red flag. All leaders have struggles, and we are commanded to be transparent on some level in safe community. Not that your leader has to tell you every single thing, but there should be depth to these accountable relationships. I've seen world-famous leaders humble themselves, reflect on their personal experience, take time to rest in hard seasons and reveal that openly, navigate personal journeys that are tough, apologize, and the list goes on. All these things should be exemplified from a healthy leader and healthy accountability relationship.

"So then, get rid of lies. Speak the truth to each other, because we are all members of the same body" (Ephesians 4:25 NIV). Let me expound on the importance of this passage in the context of accountability. Wherever there are people, there is potential for misunderstanding, lies, pain, and betrayal, and the list goes on. Some refuse to get into community because of their past experiences. Scripture is not ignorant to this reality. In fact, it directly addresses it.

Here, Paul is educating the church at Ephesus about the reality of Christian living and how to develop new relationships as a new creation. The temptation to react out of trauma from past relationships may be greater for some than others. This step in the bridge from conformity to transformation is essential. We cannot change the patterns we don't recognize. For example, when someone goes for weight loss surgery, they might be stigmatized that it is an easier route than losing the weight naturally. Actually, it has its own challenges, and I don't believe either route is easier. The person may have opted for surgery but they also need to learn a new way of doing life to maintain that progress, or the weight will come right back and even with complications.

When it comes to crossing the bridge from conformity to transformation, we learn a new way of life, and Ephesians 4 is a perfect guidebook for this process. In your time with the Lord, read and meditate on this whole chapter. I encourage you to read it often. This chapter helps us define a sense of responsibility within the context of our new life and accountability. Put off lies, and tell each other the painful truth at times. (This does not disregard tact and empathy.) Do not harbor offense. Do not keep a record of wrong (1 Corinthians 13:5). Instead, when something is stirring in your heart, go to the person and take the risk of telling the truth. Do this also in confession one to another. Do not mask or hide the truth because eventually, everything done and said in darkness comes to light.

"A stubborn fool considers his own way the right one, but a person who listens to advice is wise" (Proverbs 12:15 NIV). This is a powerful tool that really exposes how narcissistic our brains can get if we allow it. By nature, we can start to believe we are always right. We become more foolish the more right we think we are when we consider our own way to be the only right way and refuse to seek out advice, counsel, and accountability. It's not only essential to invest time and mental and emotional capacity into accountable relationships, it's foolish not to.

"The person who sins will die. A son will not be punished for his father's sins, and a father will not be punished for his son's sins. The righteousness of the righteous person will be his own, and the wickedness of the wicked person will be his own" (Ezekiel 18:20 NIV). Sometimes people avoid accountability because they develop a belief that they are bound to destruction by generational patterns or curses. This verse helps dispel the lie that we are trapped by generational trauma and demonic activity without an escape. Jesus took all our generational burdens at the cross, and any time you may see something in your life that reflects the deficits of your ancestry, you can override these patterns by acknowledging Jesus's sacrifice and your own participation in the pattern and being accountable to confess the pattern so that you don't indulge in it further in the context of community.

"Therefore, encourage each other and strengthen one another as you are doing" (1 Thessalonians 5:11 NIV).

And here's the big finale. We've discussed the importance and all the hard aspects of accountability, but in this part, we can lighten up. The confession and hard conversations are only a fraction of accountability relationships. The real end goal of accountability is to encourage and strengthen each other. This happens not only through confession, prayer, and vulnerability but also through getting to know who others are as people and who is within our communities. We can celebrate and accept each other. We can pray for each other (even when we aren't in crisis), and we can enjoy life together. Community relationships should span a variety of interests. I know communities that hunt together and communities that travel to conferences or to missions trips together. The possibilities are endless.

ONLY A SAFE CHURCH CAN OFFER ACCOUNTABILITY

I will not pretend to look the other way when it comes to reputation of the Church. Headlines of scandals and abuse do not help my cause, but I assure you, I've been impacted deeply by these events on a personal level. In 2019, we went through some of the worst experiences of our entire ministry. We found out that the ministry that had helped raise us up, the ministry that we had trusted and confided in, was doing terrible and scandalous things to people.

When some of the acts the minister we loved was committing hit the public, we stood in awe. We couldn't believe that these things could be said, let alone be true. We passionately and loyally stood for our leader, coworker, and some of our best friends. Some things that were said and done really confused us. The leader would create an apology video explaining his actions in a shifty way and then later delete it. We texted him and he responded with comments like, oh my finger slipped and I accidentally deleted the video.

My husband told me, "Something isn't right about that." Nevertheless, we had no proof and chalked it up to everything he was going through and that he needed our support and love in this difficult time. We drove hours to help maintain his church and support them the best we knew how. We made Facebook declarations of his innocence.

One night, I had a dream. I was holding a picture of my friends and us. I was crying as tear drops were falling onto the picture. A voice thundered above me. "But what if it's true, Millie?" I woke up with tears in my eyes and sweat all over my body.

"I rebuke the devil," I whispered into the room so as not to wake Rob. How dare the enemy attack our leaders is this horrible way!

A short time later, on a visit to protect and serve these same leaders, we were invited to lunch by one of the staff. This was a top-secret, confidential meeting. At the time, I didn't understand what was so top secret about it. At that table, this staff member asked us to stop talking so publicly of the man's innocence. He wasn't innocent, and the entire staff knew. He proceeded to show us evidence. My head started spinning. I felt like I couldn't breathe. We cried as we left.

I had another vision. Rob and I were walking as if through war. Casualties were all around us. I was fully awake and aware yet walking throughout the vision in real time. I could see the casualties and smell the smoke. That smell didn't leave me for years. Years later, I would be in random places and smell things burning and check my house. To this day, it still happens sometimes. It was one of the hardest times of our entire life, marriage, and ministry.

Over the next few years, I pursued my education in counseling and social work. I wanted to get to the bottom of every possible resource I could to come back strong and help serve in any and all ways to prevent this level of abuse from ever happening to others if it were at all within my power.

In that season, I reflected on the years leading to that fateful day. The signs became more clear. The grooming. Our youthful innocence. Our eagerness to be taught and trained. The public punishments if we didn't obey. The strategy of using anything we would confess against us. The pulling back and drawing close in cyclical seasons so that we responded in ways to benefit them. The taking credit for our work, taking our ideas, and using our story to make themselves seem like a hero in our lives. I had to break down and process all these instances with the Lord. There were even downright situations of assault we witnessed, but these didn't register to us because by the time we saw them, we were already trained to help instead of reaching out for help. The one time we did reach out for help from a ministry closely connected with him, they told us we were dishonoring and they wouldn't be having us back.

It was a very confusing time with this ministry, and it took years of unpacking and even some professional counseling for me to personally recover. At the time, I thought this would all be stored as a painful broken piece of my life, and now the Lord has shown me the power in Romans 8:28, that he uses all things for the good of those who love him and are called according to his purpose.

Dare I say this even applies to abusive situations? I think it could, at least it has in my life. Now I'm not saying God ordains abuse to teach us lessons. God gave man free will, and unfortunately, abuse is part of the capability of people. At the same time, I do believe that God can use everything in our story to impact the lives of others and build the kingdom of heaven.

I tell this story to show how the reality of my understanding of toxic situations and abusive dynamics. They can hinder the ability for people to receive and remain accountable. I share my story to relate to those who have been victims of abuse. In the next session, I will give what the Holy Spirit shared with me about how to identify a healthy and safe accountability atmosphere.

CHAPTER THREE
HEALTHY COMMUNITY

There's no exact combination of personality profiles or perfect framework that sets the stage for what healthy looks like within the context of community. Healthy community must include grace. Perfection only exists in grace through Jesus Christ. So when things go awry, our act of worship and praise in relationship is forgiveness and a complete wiping the slate clean. Again, I refer to 1 Corinthians 13:5 to back this up: "It [Love] keeps no record of wrong" (NIV).

However, unexpected situations happen on this earth. Logically, victims of abuse never choose it. This deep process takes place in the brain and actually changes the very wiring that dictates perception and understanding, often hindering a person from realizing what is happening to them. All that to say, God can reveal when it is happening to us like he did in my dream. Perhaps he was trying to reach me sooner, and I elevated loyalty to my leadership above my discernment and open ears to the Holy Spirit.

Both abusive and healthy communities happen in systems. Narcissistic leaders will be wired to put people in the exact roles that help facilitate and protect the abuse. This happens like a mirror image when the leader is healthy. A healthy leader gets their inspiration and strength from the Holy Spirit and the healthy leaders around them who are united on the common interests of pure and holy living. They will seek to put people in positions around them that help facilitate, protect, and enable scriptural growth.

HEALTHY COMMUNITY SYSTEMS

When I look at what it takes to build a healthy community, I refer to a concept by Murray Bowen. Family Systems Theory describes the social system within a family structure that indicates how each member impacts and influences the others.[6]

The Bible defines the Christian experience as

more than a faith, but a family. "And so that we would know that we are his true children, God released the Spirit of Sonship into our hearts—moving us to cry out intimately, "My Father! My true Father!" (Galatians 4:6).

In the context of family, the idea of community is not casual by a long shot. Family is deeply interpersonal and connected. A healthy, functioning family system needs trust. There needs to be leadership, guidance, vulnerability, and forgiveness. Every interaction and individual leaves an impact on the others. We see this in toxic and abusive families as well.

ATTACHMENT IN COMMUNITY

In my studies, I learned about the impact of attachment within family systems. We need to learn a sense of healthy attachment.

---

[6] W.H. Watson, "Family Systems Theory," Science Direct, 2012, https://www.sciencedirect.com/topics/medicine-and-dentistry/family-systems-theory.

I have even studied the idea that addiction is an attachment disorder. People who have dysregulated attachment due to childhood trauma or even more recent trauma are more likely to cope and adapt to life through an addictive mindset. An addictive mindset seeks for anything to soothe it.

This creates issues when we try to live in community. Addiction becomes a way of life, and those that fall into it usually do so innocently or not realizing that addiction is setting in. Soon enough, the hiddenness of the addiction and the shame that it fosters creates isolation. The person may start to feel unrecognizable emotions, such as aggression or irritability, especially if their secret addiction is detected or called out. Unfortunately, this happens in cycles, and each cycle that completes its rotation unhindered digs the person deeper into the addiction.

Just as we have been learning that trauma is an interruption, so is healing. For example, a healthy person is living a typical pattern in life, and some tragedy hits, causing a potential trauma. When this interruption sets in and interrupts several, if not all, areas of a person's life and the trajectory of the person's life, healing does the same thing in a holy inverted way.

Healing interrupts the unhealthy patterns and behaviors with relief, renewal, new creation identity and the mind of Christ. Jesus provided all these things at the cross of Calvary. Healing doesn't just do work within the individual; healing fixes attachment issues to others as well. We are created for connection with each other.

Whether people function in health or in dysfunction, they are hungry for attachment in a community/family setting. The hard part about dysfunction is that it sabotages attachment. If left unrecognized, it can recreate relational traumas over and over. People who learn to cope within dysfunction slowly become desensitized to their own deficits. They can develop symptoms like narcissistic traits, god-like complexes, borderline perspectives, and the list continues.

These symptoms further lead to problematic

interpersonal relationships and complex issues that otherwise take years of diagnosis and treatment to even get a handle on. Now I believe treatment is wonderful and essential for so many. Alongside treatment, Jesus Christ can interrupt anyone's life with healing. And when he does, there is fruit!

BOTH INSTANT AND PROCESS

As I stated in my first book, *Daddy Issues a New Life*, I was diagnosed with certain mood and personality disorders at a young age. Out of all the diagnosis I received, the most prominent and problematic disorder I struggled with was borderline personality disorder. I recounted the events as they unfolded in my first book. I prayed with my (at the time future) husband. I received healing in that moment. As I walked it out, I experienced the process.

In my younger, immature Christianity, I tried to define healing as an extreme in one of two categories. Is healing instantaneous, or is healing a process? After nearly two decades of ministry, I've come to find balance in the defining of terms. I now describe healing as both instantaneous and a process. We receive the healing poured out by Christ's sacrifice on the cross instantaneously.

"He himself bore our sins" in his body on the cross, so that we might die to sins and live for righteousness; "by his wounds you have been healed" (1 Peter 2:24 NIV).

As time went on, after therapy, graduation, and being off medications, I discussed how I felt the ups and downs of this experience. Going from feeling numb to experiencing emotions was a huge jump for me, and it wasn't a steady reintegration with life. This is the part I call the process.

For example, someone who commits a crime can receive healing at the cross after their crime is committed. Whom the Son sets free is free indeed. At the same time that the person is spiritually free, the person may still be imprisoned as part of the physical process due to the criminal behavior. In this context, it's easier to understand how healing is both instantaneous and a process.

When I journeyed through the aftereffects of a year of mental health medicine cocktails and intensive therapies, my emotions did fluctuate and my regulation had to adjust. In addition, I had to learn the process of applying the therapies that God used in my life without the help of medications, which was a new level of adjustment. These kinds of practicalities can be uncomfortable for people who desire an instantaneous healing process in order to avoid putting work into it. Like the example I used in the beginning of the book, a person who has weight loss surgery will still have to do the work to learn a new way of eating so as to maintain that progress.

Essentially, a person will encounter the healing of Jesus in an instant. Sometimes it's a low point in one's life where the moment of encounter with their Heavenly Father sets them radically free. In order to maintain the progress made and still function on this planet with its essence of fallen nature and factors mentioned in John 16:33, we must endure the process of learning how to exercise that self-regulation by regularly renewing our minds, setting our minds on things above, thinking on whatsoever things are true, pure, and lovely, etc.

"I have told you these things, so that in me you may have peace. In this world you will have trouble. But take heart! I have overcome the world" (John 16:33 NIV).

We cannot attempt to have a healthy attachment style within community if we aren't in the process of healing when crossing the bridge from conformity to transformation. Once we are in process, our personal desires start to become healthier. This leads to healthier common interests with others.

COMMON INTERESTS

The depth of healing we walk in will often dictate our interests. Healing can be a complex process. Some people will go through various levels of process and then need to take a step back. For some, fear of this process takes root. People can then be tempted to hold on to patterns of coping due to conformity that they are used to.

An example of this would be when someone is crossing the bridge from conformity to transformation in the area of addiction. Some people cope with life's difficult moments with alcohol. Like mental health medications, the substance regulates the person in crisis instead of the person learning how to regulate themselves. In trauma crisis, these situations can even be risky. Unlike mental health mediations, alcohol isn't prescribed nor is there accountability for it. In addition to being a poison that could kill someone in one sitting, it is completely culturally accepted and even pushed by society, making addiction almost inescapable, at least for some.

It's no wonder that when someone is making progress in abstaining from alcohol use, they may struggle to function in society. Previously, they coped via active addiction. In getting my degree in addictions counseling, I have learned that if someone slips up, we don't need to classify it as a full relapse. We can call it a *lapse*. The same is true when we backtrack from progress in our healing journey.

We may have a lapse in judgment or a lapse in behavior, but do you know who never lapses? "Jesus Christ the same yesterday, and to day, and for ever" (Hebrews 13:8 KJV).

Jesus will never lapse, even when we do. He's faithful to walk with us on our healing journey. As we walk the bridge from conformity to transformation, he is our stability. He is the foundation of our identity and attachment. We may not even fully know how to integrate and maintain healthy stable relationships, but Jesus says, "Start with me. I'm safe. I don't change. I won't trigger or abandon you. I won't harm or violate you. We will process this together at your pace. I've already taken care of the work —all you have to do is walk."

As I type this, I actually hear him speaking that over you, the reader. Read his words out loud. Write them out on an index card to place on your mirror or at your desk at work. He is speaking that over your journey.

Now that you walk this journey, this process

with Jesus through your healing, you can start to embark on healthier habits and interests. As he leads you personally, be on the search for a healthy church community. This is a huge struggle for many because some factors are beyond our control in all this. I believe we are designed for community. But how do we find a healthy one?

Like I said before, I don't pretend that every community is perfect or that abuse doesn't exist within the Church. As far as looking for a healthy community, a healthy community will have certain markers. If you have been through toxic situations within community, you will probably have a keen eye for what is unhealthy.

SIGNS TO WATCH FOR

The first thing you're going to want to do is give a lot of validity to the subtle feelings. When you feel something about a situation, I encourage you not to ignore it. After going through abuse in ministry myself, I no longer ignore that uneasy sense I get around certain people. I listen to those feelings.

Notice I said I listen to them. I acknowledge and process them. From there, I determine what to do next and set boundaries. I also debate how much I am going to allow them to dictate my decision. Notice I didn't say I allow them to control me. I allow my feelings to be felt. I allow my feelings to communicate to me, and I do not bottle them up or ignore them. This is what we need to do to walk in healthy community. Even if some of our feelings are dictated by irrationality due to traumas we are currently working through, some awareness can go a long way.

Our feelings do not have to be rational to be recognized, validated, and processed. Just because your feelings do not exactly match what you think they should be given the situation, they seldom stem from nowhere. This is called transference in counseling.

For example, in 1996, I broke my hand in gym class. Some rough kids were throwing dodgeballs, and I was sitting on the stage as I was afraid of how hard the boys would throw the dodgeballs around. Sure enough, one came darting at my face, and my hands instinctively went up to protect myself. After the blow from the ball, pain radiated through my wrist.

I would have bet any amount of money in that moment that my wrist was broken and I absolutely couldn't move it. Ironically, I could wiggle my fingers just fine. Later, in the emergency room, an x-ray showed that my right hand was actually broken between my two middle fingers. If I hadn't seen it on the x-ray, I would have had a hard time believing it. The doctors would go on to explain that pain travels within the body. We can feel the pain from our broken hand in our wrist instead of the true source.

Our emotions are much the same. Sometimes we can have a response to external stimuli that doesn't quite reflect the appropriate level of response. This doesn't mean you overreact. This means that the way the pain has transferred in your life discloses a hidden source that isn't visible to the naked eye.

Although this is actually a pain to go through,

we can be thankful when this comes to our awareness. We can dive into healing for these specific emotional reactions and uncover truth behind them. In my younger years, a therapist asked me how I was feeling. The only present emotion I could feel strongly was anger. The more he asked me what I was feeling, the angrier I got.

Finally, I admitted it to him. "I'm angry."

"Who are you angry at?"

I responded, "My father."

He went on to tell me that anger was a cover emotion. In other words, anger covers emotions like pain and disappointment.

It's important to allow our emotions to come to the surface. In some cases, this is best done in therapy. We can gain insight that helps us make sense of the things that have happened to us.

Dr. Jordan Peterson recently discussed on a TikTok that we don't have memory to pull back the past; we have memory to extract important lessons about the past.[7] Trauma often occurs when we cannot make sense of the events that have happened in our lives. Our understanding of the world around us doesn't make sense, and the very perceptions we relied on become skewed with what we have come to believe about what we experienced.

So to walk the bridge from conformity to transformation, we must be willing to face the ugly truth of what we have felt about what we have been through. There is no shortcut to this. Even receiving the instantaneous healing of Jesus, we must process the practical emotions attached to our past and current circumstances. Once we can do this, we can begin to process the inevitable challenges that come with navigating community.

---

[7] MotiveMindSetYt, TikTok, :38, July 7, 2023,
https://www.tiktok.com/@motivemindsetyt/video/7252490363393428778.

Another sign of a healthy community is one that can take on a conflict, process the emotions of those involved impartial to bias, keeping Jesus and connection at the center of the motivation. Toxic and abusive behaviors are not ignored nor are they excused. Mistakes can be made, but the specific behaviors are not normalized, which leads to repeat offenses of bad behavior against others.

Good leaders do not tear people apart, become emotionally irresponsible in their care for others, or find ways around owning their part in their mistakes. Humility is the hallmark of a good leader. Leaders are to live above reproach.

Healthy Community

CHAPTER FOUR
LIVING ABOVE REPROACH

"Appoint elders in every town as I directed you—if anyone is above reproach" (Titus 1:5–6).

In light of lots of exposure of sin and abuse in the Church, many have lost sight of what it actually means to live above reproach. This is essential if we want to discern a healthy community. The word *reproach* in that passage is ἀνέγκλητος (pronounced: anenklētos) and means "blameless" and μὴ κατηγορίᾳ ἀσωτίας ἢ ἀνυπότακτα (pronounced: mē en katēgoria asōtias, ē anypotakta). The translation here means that leaders should be not under accusation of debauchery or insubordinate.[8]

There's been a lot of confusion about the unique demographic of leadership with time and culture. As a Church, many have been so ingrained with the idea of gentle restoration, love, Matthew 18, and other concepts as it relates to interconnected relationship management. These concepts are not the same as they apply to leadership positions within the Church.

ACCUSATION OF SIN/ABUSE

We can see the standards for leadership in Titus 1 when spelled out in laymen's terms. Leaders aren't supposed to simply avoid doing bad things; they are supposed to live in such a way that they aren't even under accusation of these things. For clarity, *debauchery* means extreme indulgence in things that are pleasurable to one's body, including sexual, substance abuse, and immorality as a whole.[9]

---

[8] "Titus 1:6 Interlinear," Bible Hub, accessed January 3, 2024, https://biblehub.com/interlinear/titus/1-6.htm.

[9] Merriam-Webster Dictionary, s.v. "debauchery (n.)," accessed January 3, 2024, https://www.merriam-webster.com/dictionary/debauchery.

Today, we have many people self-educated on what they believe doctrinally rather than what Scripture actually says on these important issues. Let's clarify that leadership should never be forced. Leadership roles in any capacity are a privilege and a calling. There is a standard, though, a prerequisite, if you will, that *must* be maintained for someone to attain to and maintain a leadership role.

What is this standard? In this next section, we will lay a foundation for what leadership should look like. Many find themselves prey to poor leadership or even not upholding the standards of leadership themselves because they have been culturally impacted rather than scripturally impacted. By studying this directly from Scripture, we may even maintain a better standard for ourselves in whatever capacity God calls us to lead. Additionally, we are made aware that morality for Christians is not solely defined by our feelings that we sometimes mistake for discernment. When leaders are caught not upholding standards, for many people, emotions sometimes get in the way of leading them in the process. It's a very tricky process, and I empathize deeply, so in order to keep things crystal clear, let's define leadership morality and living above reproach according to God's Word so that there is no mincing of words or confusion.

LEADERSHIP IN SCRIPTURE

Below, we dive into an extensive list of leadership qualifications, according to the Bible. Some of these concepts are basic and aimed at foundational Christians and must be mastered with evidence through behavior and overall attitude. By mastering concepts, I don't mean a level of inhumane perfection. I mean the leader demonstrates the ability to clear these hurdles. Sometimes leaders are instated before they've worked out basic Christian characteristics. How can we expect a leader to repent and return to a healthy state of living if they've never first mastered the ability to live healthily? How can we expect leaders to be aware of those they care for if they are not first at least self-aware? Some argue about some questionable examples throughout the lifetime of David's leadership, and we will dive into that as well. But first, know that God has a clear standard for leadership. Despite human failings, God desires healthy leadership and community systems.

"But among you it will be different. Whoever wants to be a leader among you must be your servant" (Matthew 20:26). The very first point is the motive. Biblical leaders do not get into it to sooth a personal desire for fame or recognition. Leaders should not enter ministry in an effort to obtain a platform. A true leader's platform is where they place those in their care above them so they can better reach their feet for washing.

"You call me Teacher and Lord, and you are right, for so I am. If I then, your Lord and Teacher, have washed your feet, you also ought to wash one another's feet. For I have given you an example, that you also should do just as I have done to you. Truly, truly, I say to you, a servant is not greater than his master, nor is a messenger greater than the one who sent him" (John 13:13–17).

This great passage dives into a couple of dynamics of leadership, including that the position of leader is below those whom they serve. Additionally, a leader is aware of who they are and the impact they have on others. If they are not aware of how their behavior and lifestyle impacts others, then they are not actually walking out leadership. If they are found not walking in leadership, they shouldn't be coerced into it by others even if they are loved and valued. Leadership is a call from God that should be pure when evidenced in those he calls. Many will think they hear God for others, but if God has not called someone to be a servant in this capacity, they shouldn't be manipulated into it by others.

The motive for leadership should never be self-seeking even if it's the "only way the person has to make money." I've heard this argument before. But people will do serious damage to the people the leader hurts and to the leader themselves by encouraging and enabling an abusive unhealed person to move forward in their call during and through accusation of serious crimes against the body of Christ.

"Let nothing be done through selfish ambition

or conceit, but in lowliness of mind let each esteem others better than himself. Let each of you look out not only for his own interests, but also for the interests of others" (Philippians 2:3–4).

These are foundational Christian principles of how a leader should conduct themselves. Leaders are expected to be at the level of Christian faith where they have essentially mastered the basic principles of Christian living. If the leader exhibits questionable character in these basic areas regarding their faith, we must not enable that behavior.

Selfish behaviors and mindsets are not a slipup. When people continually exhibit selfish motives and actions, they are displaying what is in their heart. Again, some of these standards may feel really strict as they should be. If we raise the bar with leadership, we call people higher. People will often not challenge themselves, and where they don't, Scripture does.

"A fool vents all his feelings, but a wise man holds them back" (Proverbs 29:11). "Whoever guards his mouth and tongue, keeps his soul from troubles" (Proverbs 21:23).

This is one of the easiest ways to tell when someone is healthy. This passage is not just applicable to leadership. Anyone who has a hard time regulating their emotions will often spill out their emotions to everyone around them. Other Scriptures do give guidance on Christian health and leadership and point to the leader's responsibilities. But this verse is more of an identifying Scripture. When someone is venting without self-awareness, they may be showing signs of hunger for accountability and healing. Honestly, this can be beautiful in the context of finding the help someone needs, but for a leader, this is a major red flag. Some may think, *Oh, I can be their accountability.*

This is one of the main reasons why a leader needs to find themselves in a place of spiritual health. The moment a leader begins to make you think that you need to or are responsible for their healing, this becomes an unhealthy power dynamic.
Terminology can be confusing, especially if you've never experienced it before. We cannot

assume every broken leader is abusing others. At the same time, we can absolutely see that in some of the worst abuse cases, narcissistic leaders will always create a power dynamic by which they cannot be questioned. In addition, their deficits leave you feeling obligated and loyal to *their* process.

I address this because although it might not be popular, it must change. Let's normalize healthy leadership and stepping down (before getting entangled in sin) without penalty. Let's normalize sabbaticals and enough rest. Let's normalize ministry self-care. All these things are the leader's responsibility to manage within their lives and set appropriate boundaries even among those they serve.

"Where there is no guidance the people fall, but in abundance of counselors there is victory" (Proverbs 11:14). Even leaders need leaders. This concept is thankfully normalized in Christian culture; however, it must be said because it's not lived out as much as it's normalized. Leaders need counsel, lots of it! Leaders need guidance, lots of it! Why? Well, if this Scripture is not directly aimed at leadership, that means leaders need to be getting it themselves in a way that they also can help provide it for those they serve.

"But select capable men from all the people—men who fear God, trustworthy men who hate dishonest gain—and appoint them as officials over thousands, hundreds, fifties and tens" (Exodus 18:21). Assessment within leadership is biblical. Leaders should be honest and capable of fulfilling their roles. Once they are shown to be honest and capable, they can be trusted to lead (serve) in larger capacities.

"Be diligent to present yourself approved to God, a worker who does not need to be ashamed, rightly dividing the word of truth. But shun profane and idle babblings, for they will increase to more ungodliness" (2 Timothy 2:15–16). "And we urge you, brothers, admonish the idle, encourage the fainthearted, help the weak, be patient with them all" (1 Thessalonians 5:14).
Leaders have specific responsibilities, including a keen understanding of Scripture

(including the passages about leadership) in order to carry them out and loving them and preaching on them and discipling others. Leaders need to avoid becoming idle and lead with patience. If you are in or considering a position of leadership that God is calling you to, these are valuable insights and not mere suggestions. Master these concepts and start your leadership journey by exercising them in your everyday life.

"Remember your leaders, those who spoke to you the word of God. Consider the outcome of their way of life, and imitate their faith" (Hebrews 13:7). "In everything set them an example by doing what is good. In your teaching show integrity, seriousness and soundness of speech that cannot be condemned, so that those who oppose you may be ashamed because they have nothing bad to say about us" (Titus 2:7–8 NIV).

Leaders should live in a way that their faith can be imitated. If you notice a leader is consistently falling into sin or doing things that are not characteristic of a genuine humble leader, do not imitate them. Might I add, don't even submit to their leadership. I say this out of genuine concern for your soul and those in your care.

"Be shepherds of God's flock that is under your care, watching over them—not because you must, but because you are willing, as God wants you to be; not pursuing dishonest gain, but eager to serve; not lording it over those entrusted to you, but being examples to the flock. And when the Chief Shepherd appears, you will receive the crown of glory that will never fade away" (1 Peter 5:2–4). "Obey your leaders and submit to them, for they keep watch over your souls as those who will give an account. Let them do this with joy and not with grief, for this would be unprofitable for you" (Hebrews 13:17).

Leadership is not a scriptural mandate but a privilege with standards. Some people try to describe their calling to leadership as some kind of inescapable burden. Scripture says otherwise. This passage talks about watching over the hearts and souls of people because God wants *us* to be willing in regard to this kind of service. In fact, this privilege can and should be revoked if someone comes at it with the wrong heart and motive.

Leaders should be motivated to lead, not forced or stuck into it. Leaders should be trustworthy and examples. Be especially watchful of those who lord their leadership over others and be sure not to fall into that trap yourself. Leaders are passionate about what they do, and their demeanor and behavior reflects it.

"Behold, how good and how pleasant it is for brethren to dwell together in unity!" (Psalms 133:1).

"Pay careful attention to yourselves and to all the flock, in which the Holy Spirit has made you overseers, to care for the church of God, which he obtained with his own blood" (Acts 20:28).

This verse is separate from the section above to really express how vital it is that leaders are looking after themselves as well as others. Unhealthy leaders who justify falling into sin are not honest with themselves. When someone enters a position of leadership, they are expected and required to maintain a level of self-awareness. They should not be pitied for their bad behaviors and choices. They should also be trained to know this.

One of the main reasons we must maintain this level of standard for leadership is because leaders birth. Leaders beget other leaders. If leaders are not installed properly with training and understanding of their obligations, responsibilities, privileges, and standards, they will produce more unhealthy leaders and create community systems that protect their deficits that in time, turn into and abuse of power and of people. If we want to really discuss abuse in the church, we absolutely have to take a serious look at the level of accountability we expect as a body.

Leaders are responsible to look after themselves as well as others. It's their obligation to sit down if their life is getting out of control. It's their job to reach out for help if they are struggling. They are not a victim to ministry or stuck in ministry; they just weren't properly trained. Since improper training is often the standard, we see a lot of confusion about sin and the responsibility to handle it in leadership.

"If any of you lacks wisdom, you should ask God, who gives generously to all without finding fault, and it will be given to you" (James 1:5).

A leader should maintain an active relationship with God. There's not a ton to add to this verse as it's pretty clear. As a leader, you must have safeguards and accountability in place not only through other people but first through God himself. God never calls a leader to abuse people. If someone ever tries to convince you that they have certain sexual needs because they are a leader, that it's God's will for you to engage with them sexually, or that you must interact with them in a way that makes you feel icky because they are supposedly anointed, you need to flee that situation immediately and talk about it! God does not communicate these things. God doesn't ever ordain abuse, and I give you permission to leave those situations and talk about them, no matter what anyone says.

"Not many of you should become teachers, my brothers, for you know that we who teach will be judged with greater strictness" (James 3:1).

Scripture points out the judgement that comes with leadership, and let me tell you, it's strict! This is for good reason. This should be one of the core concepts leaders are taught before being installed. This list of scriptural expectations is not even exhaustive. If these requirements are too much for someone, that's okay. Leadership might not be in the cards for them this season.

"It is an abomination for kings to commit wicked acts, for a throne is established on righteousness" (Proverbs 16:12). "When the righteous increase, the people rejoice, but when a wicked man rules, they groan" (Proverbs 29:2).

Righteousness is the very minimal standard for those in leadership. Anything less will eventually show cracks. The Bible here says that people groan when wickedness is ruling. What's more is it's an abomination. We minimize these types of passages, but God thinks it's a very big deal. You will also notice this demeanor in a body when a leader is wicked or abusive. The evil behaviors seep into the congregation and impact others. If you see this, it could be a clue as to deeper issues in leadership. When choosing a safe community to fellowship with, be on guard for these factors.

"Be diligent to know the state of your flocks, and attend to your herds" (Proverbs 27:23).

Again, this verse points to the diligence a leader must maintain. In the exposure we went through with abusive leaders in 2019, we saw a conflict in this area. Our leader's supposed accountability proudly proclaimed how he restored our leader after his last failed marriage. After that, the only public acknowledgment he ever made was his credit for the part he felt he played in our leader's restoration to ministry. Our former leader continued in an ongoing pattern of dark nights of the soul, abuse, and even criminal behavior. Lots of this was kept from current ministry followers as he groomed and conditioned those around him to loyalty through relating his struggles and used self-pity to pull them in.

Many around the world were waiting for a statement from the man literally everyone thought our leader was accountable to. We'll call this man Johnny, but Johnny would go on to claim no responsibility for our leader. Johnny stated that he restored our leader to ministry, knowing full well his history, and released him with no public statement of not holding him accountable. He proceeded to stream rants that would go so far as to place blame and accusation on victims of abuse. This was shocking and a violation of Christian leadership.

Scripture commands leaders to be aware of those they take responsibility for. Be diligent to know those in your care, and attend to them! "If you faint in the day of adversity, your strength is small." (Proverbs 24:10). "But those who hope in the Lord will renew their strength. They will soar on wings like eagles; they will run and not grow weary, they will walk and not be faint" (Isaiah 40:31 NIV).

Struggle is part of the package that comes with leadership. It's not an endless struggle with no way out. We are given the ticket on how to handle struggle successfully. We increase in strength only through hope in the Lord. Other verses talk about how his strength is perfected in our weakness. Our strength is not based on feeling strong; it's based on our hope in him. Leaders should know how to exercise this effectively.

"A man who isolates himself seeks his own desire; he rages against all wise judgment" (Proverbs 18:1). This is a tough one because the current Western culture has made being an introvert a desired personality trait. We have whole personality tests to determine how much of our presence we feel obligated to grace others with. This is not God's desire for leadership. We must separate self-care; spiritual disciplines, such as maintaining a prayer life; and family boundaries from an introverted behavior that fosters isolation and refuses to connect with others.

And while many verses address leadership standards and approaches, there are even more.

Here are just a couple more.

"Woe to the shepherds who are destroying and scattering the sheep of my pasture!" declares the Lord" (Jeremiah 23:1).

Leadership is a very serious responsibility. Those who regularly behave in ways that cause destruction to people's lives without accountability will be held responsible before the Lord. While we can trust the justice of the Lord, we must speak up when we see destructive patterns. If you see the destroying and scattering of the sheep, do not be afraid to address it biblically. If laws are broken, do not be afraid to make formal reports within the legal system. If you are assaulted or abused or if someone is in danger, you can involve the police.

While Paul did encourage believers not to use the legal system against each other, (1 Corinthians 6:1–8), when he was wrongfully arrested and accused in Acts 21–22, Paul asks, "Is it legal for you to whip a Roman citizen who hasn't even been tried?" Paul created guidelines by which the church could settle church matters within the church if these matters didn't involve the laws of the land. This was an effort at keeping unnecessary issues outside the court systems so the testimony of believers could be preserved. However, when problems did involve the legalities of the land, Paul knew and exercised his rights to defend himself and state his case.[10]

Paul backs up his words with this Scripture: "For the authorities do not strike fear in people who are doing right, but in those who are doing wrong. Would you like to live without fear of the authorities? Do what is right, and they will honor you. The authorities are God's servants, sent for your good. But if you are doing wrong, of course you should be afraid, for they have the power to punish you.

---

[10] "What does the Bible say about lawsuits / suing?," Got Questions, accessed January 3, 2024, https://www.gotquestions.org/lawsuits-suing.html.

They are God's servants, sent for the very purpose of punishing those who do what is wrong" (Romans 13:3–4). In cases of harm and abuse, I encourage you to make a formal report to the police.

"Speak up for those who cannot speak for themselves, for the rights of all who are destitute. Speak up and judge fairly; defend the rights of the poor and needy" (Proverbs 31:8–9).

One of my all-time favorite Bible passages about leadership is a core responsibility to speak up for those who cannot speak up for themselves and their rights. Many believe we aren't to judge, which simply isn't true, but we are to judge fairly and defend the underprivileged within society.

This section reviews the many important factors when it comes to leadership structure and living above reproach. I hope this gives you a clear picture of the responsibility associated with a high position of servanthood. God takes leadership very seriously. As the verse says, it's better for a millstone to be tied around someone's neck and thrown into the sea than to lead one in your care astray. "It would be better to be thrown into the sea with a millstone hung around your neck than to cause one of these little ones to fall into sin" (Luke 17:2). This is how serious God's Word is when it comes to the power dynamic when serving vulnerable populations who respect a leader's authority as if directly from the Lord himself. Even though we know how frail a leader can be, we must acknowledge that our respect for authority creates vulnerability, and thus, when we accept a position of leadership, we remain responsible for how we influence others.

A related passage is 1 Corinthian 8:11–13. "So because of your superior knowledge, a weak believer for whom Christ died will be destroyed. And when you sin against other believers by encouraging them to do something they believe is wrong, you are sinning against Christ. So if what I eat causes another believer to sin, I will never eat meat again as long as I live—for I don't want to cause another believer to stumble." (While the direct context is in reference to food sacrificed to idols, a powerful argument is made as to the seriousness of our actions. Our actions can violate the faith of another believer and therefore must be weighed heavily.) Our leaders should go out of their way to foster a pure relationship with those they serve and facilitate a nurturing guidance to strengthen the believer's relationship with the Lord himself.

Yet another related verse, which is very similar to Luke 17:2, is Mark 9:42. "But if you cause one of these little ones who trusts in me to fall into sin, it would be better for you to be thrown into the sea with a large millstone hung around your neck." Here we see the same concept played out.

It's important to note what God is not saying in these passages:

• God is not saying abuse is okay.
• God is not saying abusers should maintain their place of authority.
• God is not saying you should hide what is happening or has happened to you.
• God is not saying that uncovering abuse is

against his plan. (Actually, he is saying quite the opposite. He says that everything said and done in darkness will be brought to light.)

"The time is coming when everything that is covered up will be revealed, and all that is secret will be made known to all. Whatever you have said in the dark will be heard in the light, and what you have whispered behind closed doors will be shouted from the housetops for all to hear!" (Luke 12:2–3).

WHAT SHOULD WE DO WHEN SOMEONE IS ACCUSED OF SERIOUS DEFILEMENT AGAINST OTHERS?

First, the victim of abuse should immediately be heard and protected. Next, depending on the severity, the incident should be reported to local law enforcement. Last, the victim should get some kind of help to process of the abuse. I always recommend professional therapy or a credible inner healing ministry, such as Mashah Inner Healing and Deliverance. (You can find out more about this ministry at MashahMinistry.com. I work on their international ministry team, have been very blessed by them, and fully endorse their framework.)

Next, depending on the church or denomination and its structure, they may have various processes to go through when reporting abuse. The first step is to validate the accusation based on the evidence. "Do not admit a charge against an elder except on the evidence of two or three witnesses" (1 Timothy 5:19 ESV).

If the person confesses the sin or if evidence shows that they have sinned, the leader must be rebuked in the presence of all. This serves as an example to others when it comes to the abuse of power against vulnerable people. They should also publicly acknowledge what they have done. "As for those who persist in sin, rebuke them in the presence of all, so that the rest may stand in fear" (1 Timothy 5:20 ESV).

Although this is not a final step, they need to continue in the correct demeanor and attitude in handling a rough situation. They must act as if they are in the presence of Jesus himself and apply these steps without prejudging or bias. "In the presence of God and of Christ Jesus and of the elect angels, I charge you to keep these rules without prejudging, doing nothing from partiality" (1 Timothy 5:21 ESV).

REPENTANCE AS IT APPLIES TO THESE SITUATIONS.

Many recount Galatians 6:1-6:

> Brothers, if someone is caught in a sin, you who are spiritual should restore him gently. But watch yourself, or you also may be tempted. Carry each other's burdens, and in this way you will fulfill the law of Christ. If anyone thinks he is something when he is nothing, he deceives himself. Each one should test his own actions. Then he can take pride in himself, without comparing himself to somebody else, for each one should carry his own load. Anyone who receives instruction in the word

must share all good things with his instructor. (NIV)

This is, of course, in reference to when a peer in the kingdom sins and how to restore them. Now our leaders are also our brothers and sister. When they are caught in sin, we must find a way to process and investigate their behavior as they are restored. One of the main questions I hear over and over is, restored to what?

However, the concern is not a restoration to ministry. This is a vast topic that varies on a case-by-case basis, but essentially, the return to ministry shouldn't even be on the table while a person is in restoration for the health of their soul. With that in mind, we should not even discuss someone's return to ministry when they are caught sinning against vulnerable people (or anyone they lead and guide).

Manipulation is a serious abuse of power, and those who abuse their call should be first concerned with genuine repentance. They should be completely removed from ministry until further notice. (And most of the time, further notice does not apply, and the removal should be permanent.)

Repentance for a fallen leader looks like getting their affairs in order, therapy, firm accountability, and possibly diving into a skill that can help them earn a living outside of ministry if they don't already have one.

Living Above Reproach

CHAPTER FIVE
TRANSFORMATION

We've addressed the following topics: trauma, the fork in the road that trauma brings us to (conformity vs. transformation), the bridge from conformity to transformation, what healthy leadership should look like, how to handle situations of abuse, and a healthy version of that process. Next, we can start to dive into the concepts of healing and transformation.

Walking from conformity to transformation can be a struggle for people who have found their survival skills in conformity. Let me reiterate that conformity is surviving by using maladaptive coping strategies that harm your well-being, body, and soul. Though you are not to be shamed for doing this, the conviction is an important part of the process. It's important to get the help you need now. Let the conviction motivate you to change. If you are addicted to substances, reach out for substance abuse help. (See the resource section in the back of this book.) If you are isolating, it's time to find community. If you are injuring yourself with forms of violence or risky sexual behaviors, seek help. Do not fear getting professional help. Even inpatient hospitalization can help people immensely. I have been there myself and would absolutely return if I needed it; I would recommend it to others too. The process is confidential.

The first step from conformity to transformation is to get stable. That means if you are in crisis or active addiction, you must get help immediately. Put the fear and cultural opinions aside. Then, start walking the process of getting firmly rooted in health and stability.

"So then, just as you received Christ Jesus as Lord, continue to live your lives in him, rooted and built up in him, strengthened in the faith as you were taught, and overflowing with thankfulness" (Colossians 2:6-7 NIV).

From conformity, we stabilize and get rooted.

In the process of rooting, we become established deeply in him. Ironically, when you've had a baby—and I've had six—one of their first instincts is called rooting. This means they use their senses to find the mothers' breast to latch on to and receive milk.

In the process of conformity, we repent, which brings us back to an infant in our walk of faith. Our first instinct should be to latch onto basic spiritual disciplines that feed us nutritional support for growth. You may be thinking, Oh yes, I'm way past this point in my walk. No, you aren't.

I am currently walking through my grad program for social work. In addition, I have been a professional life coach for years and, for decades, have worked with Christians to return them to the basics because, in time, their commitment to their own spiritual health disciplines became lost.

Some have such an extreme revelation of the finished work of the cross that it almost defiles what Jesus came to accomplish. Jesus did not take on our sin and complete the work on the cross for us to attain our own version of spiritual enlightenment that negates our responsibility or commitment to personal discipleship. Our first commitments to personal discipleship are clearly established by Jesus himself. We can look to his example for pulling away to gardens and wildernesses to navigate his relationship with the Father. Jesus, who is God himself, broke away from life to maintain a relational and private prayer life with the Father. If Jesus himself prioritized his relationship with the Father, how much more should we?

PERSONAL PRAYER LIFE

No where in the Bible does it say that the finished work of the cross negates the teachings and examples of Jesus as he walked the earth. Therefore, we must establish a private prayer life. This is probably one of the biggest struggles I see with Christians today. This should be the first concept taught to a new believer and is relevant throughout all stages of Christian maturity.

How is your relationship with the Lord? Do you have an established private time with him? I have heard some great teachings, especially for women who struggle to maintain their responsibilities and feel the presence of God while they are accomplishing household tasks like washing the dishes. This is wonderful, but don't let this idea replace the motivation to continue or establish a private and concentrated prayer life.

Follow the guidelines the Gospels lay out:

"But when you pray, go away by yourself, shut the door behind you, and pray to your Father in private. Then your Father, who sees everything, will reward you" (Matthew 6:5–6).

After repentance, prayer needs to immediately be established in the life of a believer. This order matters. The person can respond to conviction, walk out a life change, and fully enjoy the start of the private prayer life.

The establishing of a personal prayer life is also essential before navigating community aspects of discipleship. As we see, humans can be faulty. Community can be messy. We need our own relationship with the Father so that we do not confuse ourselves with our own rational explanations regarding the messes we can get ourselves into. God will reveal to us even those secrets that we cannot see.

Once we establish a personal prayer life, dive into discipleship through a local community. This can be exceptionally difficult these days for those who have felt like they've visited churches in their area that they don't align with for different reasons. I'm thankful for the internet age we live in because while I think in-person fellowship and encouragement is best, many around the world, even in places where Christianity is illegal, rely on technology to feed them spiritually. God honors and blesses this. Some pastors may struggle because they feel the technology age has made people complacent and less committed to local community. There are elements of truth to that, so when you have a solid local community, you should go in person and be committed as the Lord leads you.

HEALING IS AN INTERRUPTION

Now that you've built the foundation of your Christian walk by repenting for conforming, re-establishing a personal and private relationship with the Lord, and followed the Lord's leading by engaging with community and discipleship, the next step is diving deeper.

Years ago, I asked the Lord to reveal to me insights on trauma. During that time, he led me to understand that trauma is an interruption.

"Traumatic experiences interrupt the linear process of the complete. psychological development throughout a person's life."[11]

I wasn't even in school for mental health when the Lord showed me this, so I asked him to confirm it in Scripture, and he lead me to the foundational ministry passage that I rely on today.

"And be not conformed to this world: but be ye transformed by the renewing of your mind, that ye may prove what is that good, and acceptable, and perfect, will of God" (Romans 12:2 KJV).

We've already discussed conformity to the world, which becomes a counterfeit option for coping that slowly takes from you and increasingly traumatizes you over time. One of the most powerful words in this verse is the word *renewing*. The root word of this in English is *renewal*, and when you find out what this means, you'll never be the same. Renewal: an instance of resuming an activity or state after an interruption.[12]

When the Lord showed me this, it blew me away. I could hardly physically function; I was so overwhelmed with peace and joy. Hear me out, God has a *plan* for trauma! Trauma is no surprise to him. He can handle it.

---

[11] Vedat Sar and Erdinç Öztürk, "What Is Trauma and Dissociation?," Journal of Trauma Practice 4 no. 1–2 (November 2005):7–20, DOI:10.1300/J189v04n01_02.

[12] Oxford's Learner's Dictionary, s.v., "renewal (n.)," accessed January 3, 2024, https://www.oxfordlearnersdictionaries.com/us/definition/english/renewal.

God can handle every ugly thing we've found ourselves a victim of. He already had answers in His Word, Jesus, for trauma.

Though trauma interrupts our pattern of life, do not conform to the ways of the world. Instead, be transformed by the renewing of your mind. Here are the following words in that verse: "that ye may prove what is that good, and acceptable, and perfect will of God." Have you ever met someone who struggles to understand what the will of God is for their life? Have you ever met someone who struggles with the difference between good and bad? What about the person who struggles socially to understand what is acceptable? This person might even be you. You cognitively know the right answers at times, but your life doesn't display it. Guess what? When you see these challenges, I can trace these them back to trauma ten times out of ten. Due to trauma, we misunderstand right and wrong and become susceptible to misunderstanding the will of God for our lives.

For example, let's consider a young person who has been through a lot of abuse. They struggle with boundaries. Their brain was actually wired to believe that certain sexual behaviors are normal and a way to meet basic needs. We all have basic physiological needs, and trauma can confuse us when it comes to appropriate ways of getting our needs met.

Interestingly, in grad school, I have been studying the work of different psychological researchers. This can be a complicated concept for people in the church. Some think psychology is anti-Christian, which simply isn't true. In my studies, I have learned that some fathers and mothers in psychology developed anti-Christian theories, which is common in any secular field. At the same time, I was pleasantly surprised to find how many fathers in psychology actually came from different church denominations. Even those who strayed from their faith found themselves promoting the idea that faith is essential and not to discourage faith in the field. In fact, humans need faith. Those who lean toward atheism find themselves promoting faith in goals, careers, and accomplishments. In my opinion, this is a sad substitute and creates a very powerless faith when faith in Jesus Christ is truly life-changing. Many have seen and been impacted by the history of abuse within the Church. For this demographic, I deeply empathize. We do no justice to those in pain by invalidating their experiences, because I do understand this reality.

At the same time, psychology is not necessarily anti-faith although some demographics of the field can be. You shouldn't fear psychology in general. It's neutral in and of itself. Valid science and psychology are pro-God. Some powerful scientific and psychological arguments can lead us right to the foot of the cross, so if you can look past your own biases and embrace the idea that God uses secular studies of the body and brain to help his people mentally and physically, you have a lot to gain.

The next topic is on the work of Abraham Maslow and his chart on basic human needs. Christians sometimes seem to question what is appropriate when studying these fields. Maslow developed a chart in the shape of a triangle or pyramid. Some associate that shape with witchcraft.

While I do validate various convictions, I will not enable the extremes that come with mental illness. Out of respect for others, I will not include the graphic in this book but will describe it and credit him because this is his research. The content helps us understand how God created us with needs. At the same time, extremes can cause us to be so fearful that we cannot attain and discern basic knowledge. This can actually be symptomatic of some illnesses that can eventually lead to isolation. So while I never intend to purposely trigger anyone, let this information stretch you. Line all things up with God's Word and follow the Holy Spirit. If you are fearful, it might be time to schedule inner healing and deliverance. (Seriously, again. This is another shameless plug for Mashah inner healing and deliverance.)

UNDERSTANDING OUR BASIC NEEDS

In order to walk in transformation, we need to understand that God created us with basic needs. Famous American humanistic psychologist Abraham Maslow researched basic human needs and developed a descriptive chart. On the most foundational level, we have physiological needs: breathing, food, water, sex, sleep, homeostasis, and excretion. If these basic needs aren't met, they will take a toll on our long-term health.

Matthew 6 talks about some of these needs in connection with not worrying.

> Therefore I tell you, do not worry about your life, what you will eat or drink; or about your body, what you will wear. Is not life more than food, and the body more than clothes? Look at the birds of the air; they do not sow or reap or store away in barns, and yet your heavenly Father feeds them. Are you not much more valuable than they? Can any one of you by worrying add a single hour to your life?
>
> And why do you worry about

clothes? See how the flowers of the field grow. They do not labor or spin. Yet I tell you that not even Solomon in all his splendor was dressed like one of these. If that is how God clothes the grass of the field, which is here today and tomorrow is thrown into the fire, will he not much more clothe you—you of little faith? So do not worry, saying, 'What shall we eat?' or 'What shall we drink?' or 'What shall we wear?' For the pagans run after all these things, and your heavenly Father knows that you need them. But seek first his kingdom and his righteousness, and all these things will be given to you as well. Therefore do not worry about tomorrow, for tomorrow will worry about itself. Each day has enough trouble of its own. (Matthew 6:25–34 NIV)

God provides our basic needs and worrying about them won't help us in the long term. At the same time, we are allowed to assess our basic physiological needs and bring them before the Lord if we feel, in a practical sense, that we are lacking. For example, a controversial one is sex.

Sex is a basic physiological need, especially within the context of marriage. The Christian conviction is that sex is exclusively reserved for the boundaries of a committed marriage relationship and is not to be exercised outside that. This is why celibacy is a calling because sex and sexuality are core parts of who we are. Sex is not evil—it's beautiful when, like all basic needs, it is met appropriately.

However, not all needs are dependent on our actions alone. Concepts like sex and homeostasis have to do with our relationships. Marriages hopefully navigate the waters of a sexual life together. They have to define their boundaries and convictions based on Scripture. Even within the context of the Bible, the spectrum of belief can vary. This need cannot be satisfied alone. Sometimes in order to improve our sex life in our marriage, we have to scale back with our partner and asses a variety of factors. Here, Christian marriage and family counselors can be a huge asset.

Even though God provides all we need within reach, we do not have to fear a lack of provision, but we must manage it. We are called to be good stewards according to the Word. So we must take into consideration how we get our needs met. If your basic need for sex is not getting met in your marriage, please consider counseling to help align goals and expectations in your relationship. I may expound on this topic in the future. This is an area with many topics that we could address. But since this book does not exclusively focus on marriage, I will save if for another day.

The point, though, is God provides our needs even in relationships with others, but we must be able to assess if our needs are being met and recalibrate through stewardship of the many gifts He gave us, such as marriage. Marriages are a beautiful gift but must be stewarded well. We must be sure that we are planting good seeds in good soil so that we bear good fruit.

Once our basic physiological needs are met, we can move to the next stage of need: safety.

Safety includes security of body, employment, resources, morality, the family health, and property. This is where it gets tricky, because if the first group of physiological needs isn't met, you may actually function in the safety category for a short time. A ridiculous example would be if you aren't breathing, you may still attain a sense of morality. At most, a person can only survive four-to-six minutes without air. If something cuts off your air supply, that's about how long you have to figure out what's doing it and get help so that you can breathe again.

When we were kids, most of us had contests to see how long we could stay underwater and hold our breath. If someone lasted close to a minute, they seemed to have some special God-given ability. In that first minute, you maintain a sense of morality. You're playing a game. But if your air supply is cut off much longer, your mentality might start to change. You might see someone's leg under the water. You might start to pull on the leg, not knowing if it's actually pulling the other person under in order to pull yourself to the surface. This is human instinct. If you're underwater and get stuck there, you will start doing whatever you can in order to survive as your body starts going into panic mode.

You may even do things that would shock you. You might not be thinking you are pulling someone under, but your basic need for air isn't being met, so your only concern is for the next breath. Morally, in your right mind, you would never pull someone underwater to save yourself, but in the frantic effort to survive, your next thought is only that next breath.

I cannot possibly think of a better explanation for trauma than this. Trauma interrupts how you would normally process your behaviors and thoughts and puts you in survival mode for your basic physiological needs. You cannot even function at the safety level because your basic physiological needs aren't being met and therefore, your safety is threatened. As we renew our minds, God brings us to our basic physiological needs. Notice that one of those basic physiological needs is homeostasis or stability, equilibrium, and peace.

Before I continue to the next levels, let me

reiterate that we must have our needs met in this specific order. Once our physiological needs are met, we are capable of managing a level of safety that facilitates security of body, employment, resources, morality, the family health, and property. When our physiological needs are met, we begin to think about ways to continue to meet those needs. Employment is a great example of this. Many struggle to understand why the homeless population doesn't just get a job. But there is much more to it than that.

When I was homeless as a late teen, I was fortunate enough to be able to stay in a homeless shelter and gain access to showers and the meals they would offer there. Most homeless people don't even have access to these basics, and most shelters limit how long you are allowed to stay. So if a homeless person does not have access to self-care, not many places will hire that person who cannot take care of basic hygiene. Additionally, some are suffering psychologically with issues like PTSD so that even if they had shelter, food, and water, their overall homeostasis is consistently interrupted with fear, terror, and aggression. Furthermore, statistics show that 25 to 30 percent of homeless individuals struggle with serious mental illnesses. In addition, homelessness exacerbates mental illness, so you then have a vicious cycle.[13]

These factors create an environment that is not conducive to success in society. We need better resources for this population, and I couldn't be more proud of the church when they develop and offer much-needed services to this population. It touches my heart since I experienced this personally.

Once our physiological and safety needs are met, we can then move into the areas of friendship, family, and sexual intimacy. We can focus on these relational aspects because we feel stable enough that our basic needs are met and safe enough that we can control the external environments so that we can develop relationships.

---

[13] Deborah K. Padgett, Homelessness, housing instability and mental health: making the connections,"
BJPsych Bull, 44, no. 5 (October 2020):197–201, doi: 10.1192/bjb.2020.49.

Notice that sexual intimacy is mentioned here, and sex is mentioned as a basic need at the first level. Because sex alone is not necessarily healthy and does not necessarily contribute to the overall health of a person. Sexual intimacy is developed within relationship (marriage) as a process and is a journey that takes communication, exploration, discovery, navigating, and so much more. It's a much more complex process than just the basic need for sex. Again, that topic is more geared for marriage but is a great example of how complex we are as people.

At this level, we may also realize our need for community. We may see people at our previous level of safety when cultivating our career goals and employments as part of security, but coworkers don't necessarily equate to the level of intimacy that we need in the love and belonging category, the category above safety. After our basic needs and safety are in place, we can dive into community. We desire relationships that many communities define as doing life together. Many find lifelong partners in community and best friendships. Many raise their children in communities and celebrate major life milestones together.

We naturally look for and connect with others deeply and intimately. God designed us as a body, which is the exact description the Bible uses to describe the connection between his children. How deeply and intricately connected is the body? First Corinthians 12:24 says, "Can the hand say to the foot it doesn't need it?" Absolutely not. They are equally essential to the functioning of a body in homeostasis.

When trauma occurs within community, this threatens the level beneath community (love/belonging) and even threatens safety. Trauma includes the violation of boundaries, hurtful words, and confusion and division. This threatens all involved.

At this point, people start reacting within their preset trauma responses. Many feel they have to pick a side and decide who is right and who is wrong. Often, people will rely on their personal history to come to these determinations. That's why it's important to look to Scripture with the best knowledge we have and remain humble and prayerful in these horrible situations. Never shame someone who comes forward with a story. If the situation involves illegal activity, the answer isn't Matthew 18. The answer is the police station, and we've already gone over a lot of that protocol in this book, especially when it comes to the abuse of power in leadership. God's Word is clear on the standards for leadership. You are not being disloyal or unbiblical by bringing your suspicions to the law.

For clarity, I'm specifically addressing abuse, trauma, and even illegal behavior in the church. We have enough books and teaching on offense and forgiveness. We need spiritually sensitive, wise standards in handling serious allegations that do not fit into the offense category. Abuse and offense are not the same thing. Abuse can cause offense, but when handled correctly, the safety of people should not be threatened by those they trust.

One of the top bad press issues in the church is scandal and abuse. We mustn't ignore these issues any longer. When we begin to handle matters correctly, we can promote a greater sense of safe community. If you have had negative experiences in the church, it's not in your head. You are not alone. To maintain a sense of depth in your Christian walk, you need others, and you still need community. We need community but not only surrounding what we enjoy. We need community surrounding us that helps sharpen our faith in ways that are natural to us.

Some people believe the answer is to destroy the church structure to self-protect from their experiences of pain and abuse at the hands of another in a church setting. However, this is a gray area. Some of these claims regarding church organizational problems are certainly accurate. At the same time, certain structures can benefit facility maintenance and events that help draw people together so that they grow. I'm neither for or against this idea; I just validate it as a response many have, especially in these generations.

God uses structure, and He uses unstructured faith as well. He uses all of it in the context of community far more than we know. I have faith in a big God, one who is far greater than my understanding. So let the Holy Spirit lead you in the way that you can be lead. If He leads you to a house church, go there. You don't need to demonize the concept of a structured church. And if you are lead to a structured church, you don't need to demonize a house church or people who gather together and fellowship regularly in an irregular structure. The bottom line is, let him lead you to and through community. Allow yourself to heal from your past, and don't do it in isolation if at all possible.

The level after love/belonging is esteem and encompasses self-esteem, confidence, achievement, and respect of and by others. Have you ever met someone who is extremely negative? They might need a friend because their love/belonging needs aren't being met. Their marriage might be struggling. (But that might not necessarily even be your business if you aren't trained and called to help them. You would do help them more by praying for them and asking God how you can support them. Some people just need a date night and a sitter.)

Perhaps their deficit stems from deeper and more basic unmet needs. Community is a great place for someone to access what they need on a basic level, such as safety and physiological needs. In the context of community, people can gain confidence, self-esteem, respect, and so much more.

The last category is where we have fun. People often desire to be creative and moral, releasing themselves in expression and birthing creativity. This category includes morality, creativity, spontaneity, problem solving, lack of prejudice, and acceptance of facts. We all know people who lack a sense of morality or who can't accept facts. We've all met people who struggle with this. At times, we have been those people. It simply means the person has deficits in other basic areas. By taking these things into consideration, we may have more grace for ourselves and others who struggle.

When we take care of our needs, this can make all the difference in our health and the health of others. Understanding our needs can help us better understand the transformation processes by the renewing of the mind.

As I mentioned earlier, Romans 12:2 addresses how the renewing of our minds affects our ability to understand and know the good and perfect will of God for our lives. That's because the renewing of our minds with God's truth brings us what every basic need. Our need for intimacy with God is a basic physiological need. Once this need is met, all the rest of our needs will be provided. We can also work on deficits we may not even know we have. The renewing of our minds helps us develop our sense of safety, love and belonging, esteem and self-actualization.

I encourage you to go through the lists and ask the Holy Spirit to open your eyes to deficits in your basic needs. In what areas do you have basic needs that aren't being met and what levels above those are being impacted? An example would be if you struggle with low self-esteem, you may have a hard time being creative in your desire to become an entrepreneur. In what ways does the Holy Spirit need to work in your life to provide what you need overall?

Transformation

TRUST

When working with couples, there will often be a presenting problem in a counseling setting. One of the first things that's important for the couple to do is clearly define some of the core issues. After the issues are identified, each person must learn how to take ownership in the areas of deficit. When we own our part in how we got to where we are today, only then can trust be rebuilt in transparency. This will facilitate a renewed healthy relationship framework. This concept also works in the context of rebuilding identity through relationship with God alone.

Going through trauma and abuse can make trust for self and others very difficult in the aftermath. One of the reasons for this is because before the trauma, you maintained a sense of reality that after the trauma, you realized wasn't completely true. When you come to find out that the world around you seems to be untrue, this creates inconsistencies in your belief patterns. You learn that anything you believe can be untrue at any time, so you set up safeguards to jump ship when something seems off. This might lead you to become hypervigilant and reactive instead of responsive in the context of relationship. You may feel as if your trust is permanently broken.

Once you have gone through the process of realizing the trauma and accepting and working through some of the core components that shifted your life so dramatically, you will notice areas of distrust rise to the surface. You may move on to new relationships, but inside, you question their authenticity or loyalty. You have these internal invisible battles that take a long time to work through. You may overreact to what would otherwise be considered mild conflicts.

The steps to and through healing are not always linear. I will keep returning to the concept that just as trauma is an interruption, so is healing. At one time, you were happy and stable, and the shift happened that turned everything upside down. That's the trauma. Now, we need an earthshaking shift to occur again that breaks all those fearful mindsets and resets all that beautiful vulnerability that God has instilled in your mind. Without this vulnerability, you will struggle to process much of what you endured. You'll come to a resolution, but you'll conclude that you learned something negative about people and life. That conclusion won't always serve you. In fact, it may get you by for a short season, but it will always serve as an offense to where God is calling you.

I can say this confidently because trust is the very building block of relationships, and if that is overlooked and replaced with cognitive rules that keep you safe from replaying traumatic events, they will eventually invite you to conform to the patterns of the world. Trust is a step in the road between conformity and transformation. There's no way around it. When we take the step of trust, we might have to face a lot of ugly experiences and beliefs about others. For some, this is a great time to invest in counseling, coaching, or inner healing. As we become vulnerable to what we've come to believe as a result of trauma and abuse, we must be careful to replace those negative cognitive sensibilities with heavenly truths.

Cognitive sensibilities are what we come to believe in order to make sense of the secular world around us based on relevant history. Human nature analyzes patterns and tries to make sense of them. Unfortunately, the cognitions developed as a result of trauma don't always make sense for our overall health. The only thing that can break those cognitive rules we develop are heavenly truths. We exercise these tools to rebuild trust in our lives. After devastation, we lose a sense of trust and not just for others. We first lose it for ourselves. We may have been told and believed horrible things about ourselves. You might even have some evidence that some of those horrible things that you were told about yourself are true. These words and labels have taken deep root in your heart. If you think that you have already worked through your trauma and can believe good things about others but still carry a sense of self-hatred with you, don't be deceived. You cannot progress past the level until you reframe your negative view of yourself and develop God's perspective.

You may read think that you just cannot succeed in this area. I can tell you that you can. It takes time and patience. We need to use that burning that rises to the surface when we discuss these topics. In time, you will build trust with yourself. Some may even need to build trust with God, and I assure you, despite what you may have been told, that's okay. God is not insecure when we need to take the time to work through this process. He can handle us at our best and at our worst.

So in this next phase, we will assess and process the depth of trust we carry for God, ourselves, and others.

> Trust in the Lord completely, and do not rely on your own opinions. With all your heart rely on him to guide you, and he will lead you in every decision you make. Become intimate with him in whatever you do, and he will lead you wherever you go. Don't think for a moment that you know it all, for wisdom comes when you adore him with undivided devotion and avoid everything that's wrong. Then you will

find the healing refreshment your body and spirit long for. Glorify God with all your wealth, honoring him with your firstfruits, with every increase that comes to you. Then every dimension of your life will overflow with blessings from an uncontainable source of inner joy! (Proverbs 3:5–10 TPT)

IS TRUST A CHOICE?

This is a tricky question. Typically, within the context of relationship, trust is built over time and based on behavior. When building trust in human relationships, we do not need to choose to trust someone who has not earned our trust with their behavior. In abusive relationships, we are often taught to overlook actions and make the choice to trust no matter what. So after abuse, we may decide that no one is worth trusting, no matter their behavior.

Sometimes people stop trusting God based on the actions of others. It's especially dangerous for the individuals who have caused or who are causing harm. As we've discussed, it's better for a millstone to be tied around the neck of an abuser who leads little ones (or vulnerable people who trust them) astray. God takes this very seriously because those who carry titles in ministry represent him. So when they abuse others, it's as if God is doing it from the victim's perspective.

In order for us to come to a place of honesty as to what caused our distrust, we must place the actions of the perpetrator in the right place. This may take genuine reflection to discover what is at the root of the distrust. Think of a time when you used to trust. When did it change? You may start reflecting on points in your life where people behaved in ways that cut into your heart. These are key moments. These memories that come to the surface, these moments of trauma, need to be addressed so that you can move forward. This is the source of the distrust. You may have made peace with the events themselves. You may have come up with explanations and deeper lessons from these experiences that help you function in day-to-day life. The next step is breaking down the lost trust that occurred in the process.

Below, take a moment to process the events themselves. If you don't have enough space here, get a composition notebook and continue processing there. If you are currently in therapy, you may want to take this to the therapist for your next session. If you are considering therapy, this could be a great first step. Write out your thoughts and bring the journal to your first session. The more detail you give, the better. The limited space here is not indicative of how short or long this should be. You may not want to write in this book if others will have access to it now or in the future.

When did your distrust begin? What events surrounded this moment? Process this well. Write out details in a safe book that you hide or consider burning in the future.

_____
_____
_____
_____
_____
_____

That was heavy. You may be questioning if these events were enough to cause the level of distrust you carry. The answer to that is absolutely yes. They were enough. There's no wrong way these hurtful events impacted you. It's not you, your reaction, or your processing that's wrong. But the offense against you was wrong. Now we're getting to the bottom of the events that developed unhealthy perspectives in your life. Until these events are uncovered as deeply and as many times as they need to be uncovered, they will fester inside you. Remember, this might not be a onetime process. These events sometimes have layers that you need to remove one at a time. Give yourself space and time to do this.

In other words, process with this exercise as many times as you need to. Write your story over and over and over. Get journals specifically for this purpose. Do not believe that at some point, you must forcefully shut yourself down. As long as there's an urge to process, do it.

The next step is assessing God's part in the process. I have a teaching on my website called "Where was God when I was abused?" I asked the Lord for this revelation when I was processing my own journey. When I help others, this is one of the most pivotal questions that people ask.

People often want to know why God didn't stop the abuse. I'm not going to pretend to have all the answers, but here is some insight God showed me that helped me come to a place of peace with the actions of others. We've all heard of the free-will argument. If God forced us to be good people, there would be no room for authentic love. I didn't make those rules, but I do know that's the most popular argument for how and why God is present with us during abuse and doesn't strike our abuser dead because of their actions.

At the same time, this free-will argument doesn't just make the pain go away. It doesn't necessarily reestablish our trust with the Lord. So when I asked God for insight to teach on where He was during our abuse, I had a vision. In my vision, I saw the crown of thorns dug into his head as he was hanging from the cross of Calvary. Where was God when we were abused? He was there, hanging from the cross in excruciating pain.

> So let us stop going over the basic teachings about Christ again and again. Let us go on instead and become mature in our understanding. Surely we don't need to start again with the fundamental importance of

repenting from evil deeds and placing our faith in God. You don't need further instruction about baptisms, the laying on of hands, the resurrection of the dead, and eternal judgment. And so, God willing, we will move forward to further understanding.

For it is impossible to bring back to repentance those who were once enlightened—those who have experienced the good things of heaven and shared in the Holy Spirit, who have tasted the goodness of the word of God and the power of the age to come— and who then turn away from God. It is impossible to bring such people back to repentance; by rejecting the Son of God, they themselves are nailing him to the cross once again and holding him up to public shame. (Hebrews 6: 1–6)

In this passage, we can see that God is not permitting those who reject God to abuse us. Instead, they repeatedly nail him to the cross. When we are abused, Jesus is suffering the excruciating pain of his crucifixion over and over.

While this still doesn't make the abuse easy to understand, we can follow the advice of Proverbs 3:5–6, trust in the Lord, and lean not on our own understanding. This is specifically why I wanted revelation from the Lord on this topic.

When I was sixteen years old and in desperate need of emotional and spiritual help, a youth pastor had me join her in private prayer sessions. She asked me to think about abusive memories and then picture Jesus there. When I couldn't see him there, she kept pressing. We would wait for hours at times, asking for Jesus showed up. My natural imagination is not vivid at all. So I eventually had to come to the place where I forced myself to picture him in the room during my abuse. But this did not bring me peace. In fact, I felt all the more he may have been inactive and distant.

Recently, I asked him if this model was healthy. He then showed me that He was on the cross, which made a lot more sense. I stand by this. Jesus is not in the corner of the room watching your abuse with a tear in his eyes, helpless and inactive. Jesus was in excruciating pain at the cross of Calvary, relating to the cost of free will of man.

At times, God will lead you to revisit memories of abuse. This varies by person and certainly isn't for everyone. I can't speak for every ministry that practices various methods of inner healing. However, I can say that inner healing is safest in the presence of a trusted and reputable mental health professional. They do exist in the church and are becoming more popular as people within the church advocate for the normalization of proper self-care with professional help.

HEALING AND TRUST

Healing and trust are connected, especially when it comes to repairing our walk with the Lord after abuse. Not everyone struggles in this way. For many, their relationship with the Lord is the reason they can walk through abuse and persevere. The ultimate sacrifice for the sins of humanity didn't only account for our sins but also the sins of our abuser and not so that they can act and remain unaccountable and continue to hurt others. We must separate the issues into the appropriate categories. We must place blame where true blame is due. For the person who acted against us, we must realize that they committed the crime and not the Lord. We need to restore our trust with the Lord so that we can make progress in our walk with Him.

"When the righteous cry for help, the Lord hears and delivers them out of all their troubles. The Lord is near to the brokenhearted and saves the crushed in spirit. Many are the afflictions of the righteous, but the Lord delivers him out of them all. He keeps all his bones; not one of them is broken" (Psalm 34:17–20 ESV)

TRUST WITH YOURSELF

Next, we need to face the trust issues we have with ourselves. One of the keys to this is noticing what you believe about yourself and if you trust yourself. Abuse directly correlates to how we feel about ourselves, especially if we repeatedly endured complex trauma. We might think we are dumb because we fell for the tricks others played on us. We then develop thought patterns that we cannot trust ourselves to be smart enough to handle relationships. We may also believe we aren't worthy of trusting ourselves. Unfortunately, even if we live in positive regard and admiration for God, our self-hatred is still enough to destroy our lives.

> So I hated life, because what is done under the sun was grievous to me, for all is vanity and a striving after wind. I hated all my toil in which I toil under the sun, seeing that I must leave it to the man who will come after me, and who knows whether that person will be wise or foolish? Yet they will have control

over all the fruit of my toil into which I have poured my effort and skill under the sun. This too is meaningless. So my heart began to despair over all my toilsome labor under the sun. For a person may labor with wisdom, knowledge and skill, and then they must leave all they own to another who has not toiled for it. This too is meaningless and a great misfortune. What do people get for all the toil and anxious striving with which they labor under the sun? All their days their work is grief and pain; even at night their minds do not rest. This too is meaningless. A person can do nothing better than to eat and drink and find satisfaction in their own toil. This too, I see, is from the hand of God, for without him, who can eat or find enjoyment? (Ecclesiastes 2:17–25 ESV)

Not much screams depression like the book of Ecclesiastes. Here, we see the result of abuse over time without healing. We see an invitation to conformity. Unchecked pain turns into a hatred for life because our very existence becomes chronically painful. The ways people find to cope outside of Jesus will lead to death ten times out of ten.

As the passage progresses, we see that we determine the direction of our lives by how we process and let go of offensive acts against us. If we fail to process these events correctly, life starts to lose meaning and purpose. We lose passion for all that God has already accomplished in us. In this passage, as the Lord leads us through this process, he lets it all out without filter. This is essential. Then, through the processing (all of which God is more than capable of handling), he is ultimately led back to thankfulness to the Lord, for he realizes that only through God will he survive what he has experienced.

Even if you've strayed for a time, run to him, for only there will you find your healing and hope of enjoyment in life again. The trauma will not outlast the strength he can provide if we are willing to use every bit of that strength. We must be honest about it, though.

As a former fitness coach, I found that people can be convinced to do more than they think because our brains are preset to feel maxed out before we actually are. We can actually tell our brains that we will not give up even when our body feels like we have no other choice. I also apply this concept to healing from abuse and trauma. You may struggle with self-hatred. You might not be able to get out of bed. Your limbs might not move. Your heart might race when you try.

I'm now your spiritual fitness coach. You can't move? It's okay. *Do it anyway. Get up. Get out of bed. Get on the internet and find a mental health provider on your insurance plan. If you don't have insurance, call some who accepts payments on a sliding scale. If you can't afford it, ask for help. Start a GoFundMe. I'd rather contribute to your GoFundMe for therapy than attend your funeral.*

See, the italics here are intentional. I'm begging and pleading for you to do whatever you have to do to get that dark cloud you are carrying covertly and functioning under exposed for your own good in a safe environment so that it can loosen its grip on your soul. Ask for help from friends and family too. Do what it takes to work through the parts of you that hate yourself. If you don't, the results can be fatal, and I speak from experience. Don't lose hope. But if you have lost hope, that's okay. Just focus on step one: Reaching out for help.

Here, we are not addressing your struggle with self-hatred. You may not have even been honest with yourself about it. It comes out in subtle comments when you look in the mirror or make a mistake. What statements do you mutter in these instances? You see? We all leak what we really believe about ourselves, but you will never be able to address it if you are not honest about it. Below, I want you to describe what you feel about yourself. (And I encourage a separate journal for extensive writing on this issue as well.) Don't correct your feelings with truth according to Scripture. Don't mix up the process. We must expose the truth first, then we can correct our beliefs. For now, you may be in a dark place. This process may be triggering, so make sure you are in a safe place where you can freely cry. You might want to do this step on the weekend. When you invest your time and energy into therapeutic practices, you sometimes feel worse before you even start to feel better.

Now be truthful. Drop your self-protection because it's only protecting the toxic beliefs at this point. What is the ugly truth about yourself?

_____
_____
_____
_____
_____
_____
_____
_____
_____
_____
_____
_____
_____
_____
_____

Transformation

Once you finish the above activity, put this book down, and feel the feelings. Put worship on, punch a pillow, scream, scribble, rip up paper or tissues, cry, and turn up the worship music even louder. Do not pretend to control this process. You are *in* process right now as you read these words. The more you allow yourself to feel and embrace the expression of your emotions, the more successful your process will be. Do this until you start to calm down and feel waves of relief. At that point, you may be tired and need to rest. The Lord may also reveal truth to you about your identity or how he feels about you. Write them in the section below or in your journal.

_____
_____
_____
_____
_____
_____
_____
_____
_____
_____
_____

Congratulations! Some of these concepts are not answers for your pain or to tell you how to deal with what you have been through. Some of these things are simple: how to uncover the deeper issues and process them the only place you *will* find answers, in Jesus himself!

If you have endured serious and complex trauma with symptoms of self-hatred, you will need to do this process as many times as the Lord leads you to do so. Keep your journal handy and protected. Your process is not anyone else's business, and at the same time, I encourage you to find those you can be accountable to on your journey as defined within the context of healthy relationship. This was discussed earlier in this book.

The purpose for this part of the process is that you will never be able to build a sense of trust within yourself until you are vulnerable and assess the pre-existing pain caused by the traumas. Now I can list tons of Bible verses on identity that you can pray and meditate on, but we all have Google. We can look up those verses that best apply to us. Self-hatred and low self-esteem are separate from each other although they are connected. In order to overcome self-hatred, the pain and truth must be exposed and processed safely.

Bring this information to your therapist or inner healing team. Sometimes when we are in therapy, we tend to wait until the session to remember the important matters we want to talk about and may even feel fine the day of our appointment. These exercises and your process are great to bring to session.

REBUILDING TRUST WITH YOURSELF

You are doing the very first thing necessary to rebuild self-trust. For a long time, in the context of self-hatred, we are not honest with ourselves. We tell ourselves we are fine and also that we are ugly, stupid, and worthless. Well, that's clearly a lie because those two statements directly contradict each other. If we are ugly, stupid, and worthless, we are obviously not fine. So becoming honest that we are not okay facilitates the uncapping of the deeper thoughts we need to process.

In the next session, the identity that needs to be restored in your life can only come by revelation. If you struggle with this next part or can't navigate it at all, go back to the previous section. Keep working through the previous section until you can complete the next part.

In this section, I want you to start writing what God has said over your life and about who you are. You may experience resistance here. It's a long jump from self-hatred to hear the truth of your identity. I don't want you to regurgitate Scripture here, though the truth of your identity should be confirmed with the Word. Instead, close your eyes and block out the world around you.

Ask God genuinely and sincerely, what is the *actual* truth about me?

_____
_____
_____
_____
_____
_____

Transformation

This process, like the process before, should be repeated regularly as well. Even if he revels the same truths to you and you rewrite them over and over, do it. God is actually bringing you on a healing journey, and it is effective even if it seems redundant.

All that we've discussed so far in this book was leading to the processes you have just completed. I'm incredibly proud of you for putting in the work thus far. I have been there myself and know the work it takes to process this way. It's no simple task. It's a thankless bravery that many might undermine when they don't understand it. So I want to acknowledge your courage. I'm proud of you and thankful you are here reading this. I look forward to your testimony, and if you find me on social media or via my contact info in the back of this book, I look forward to hearing how God has brought you through this process using these methods.

BUILDING TRUST IN RELATIONSHIPS

You may have thought you'd never get to this

pivotal moment again. You may have even sworn off relationships and made certain promises out of self-protection. But God has better plans for you than any of the safeguards you've developed to protect yourself. The previous exercises in building trust with God and self are a prerequisite to building healthy trust in relationship with others. We must have a sense of identity in order to partake in a give-and-take relationship with others. Abuse travels in cycles through relationships that take from others and self-protect. It's how we become like those who have hurt us.

We must realize that our relationship with God and our identity cannot be sourced from our traumatic experiences. Now that we've done some exercises to expose our pain and process in the presence of the Lord and hopefully with accountability of trusted others, we can enter community relationships with healthy contributions. Our motivation for trust with others is not to extract from people what we should be getting from God. We must be sure our motivation in relationship is truthful. If we only reach out to those for what we need and then blame them for not filling spaces in our lives impossible for them to meet, we run a great risk of becoming abusers ourselves. This may have been done to you, but if you want to stop the cycle of abuse, you must heal and relate to others in a healthy way. Relationships require trust, and trust is built over time.

I was once a student in a ministry school where the leader was later exposed for being a predator. I had received a scholarship, and the male leader took more interest in me than in my husband. I chalked it up to his passion for empowering women in ministry. I was wrong as I would find out much later. In this instance, I was a target, and the Lord preserved me when the school was exposed just before I was about to purchase tickets to attend the graduation.

After the exposure and as I processed these events, I noticed some dangerous and unhealthy concepts being taught in the school as part of the grooming process. Some of these twisted concepts included not avoiding the appearance of evil, avoiding suspicion, and family roles.

The leader had courses on how everything

we've been taught about certain Bible passages was wrong and that these passages meant something completely different in the original Hebrew and Greek. The arguments were convincing, and it never occurred to me that someone would use the Bible to groom people for personal sexual exploitation, but this was exactly what was happening. We were taught that the appearance of evil referred to the concept of avoiding the appearance of witchcraft and not to be overly fearful of being seen with a member of the opposite sex and so forth. This worked out perfectly so that he could then take women to a movie and assault them under the guise of a fatherly type of relationship.

He addressed the very famous Christian concept of side hugs and said there was no need for this level of hypervigilance. He suggested that everyone hugged normally and that "to the pure, all things are pure." In other words, if a regular hug was questionable for you, then you must not be "pure," so the problem was with you. This, too, gave more leeway for his predatory behaviors. Finally, he extensively addressed avoiding the spirit of suspicion.

He was grooming us. So all these teachings made sense to the students because we *were* mostly pure hearted. While hearing about them without context seems strange, it didn't seem weird to us as students. After his exposure, we learned he was crossing boundaries and grooming students to accept his boundary pushing. We were all very shocked. I was personally puzzled as I processed how he did this in such a calculated way. I struggled to believe a lot of what had happened. Then, a well-known minister and licensed clinician in the mental health field was called into the situation to address the concerns. The leader was diagnosed with narcissistic personality disorder. Many of us were confused because we heard different conflicting reports about the leader's progress.

For instance, we were told that he was not to contact any students from the former school. But next, the leader would get on Facebook live and cry and pull on our heartstrings to that we all felt bad for him. It was so difficult to process.

When you've been through this type of spiritual abuse, it only makes sense that your trust and interaction with community becomes conflicted. But I still believe there is always hope.

HOPE FOR THE ABUSIVE LEADER

When cases of abuse emerge from the church, the entire church system tends to react in fear. People struggle with the fear of false accusation. Let me tell you, false accusation does exist, and it is absolutely terrible. God is not for false accusation. All throughout God's Word, you can see instruction on what to do in the case of false accusation. I highly recommend doing a topical Bible study on this subject if you are facing it in your own life. At the same time, assuming a victim with an alleged accusation of serious abuse is falsifying their story is wrong on many levels. We are often in denial about these matters due to our fear and discomfort. Initially, our disappointment in leadership that betrays us may manifest as denial. So when we experience this, we need to take it to the Lord quietly. When someone is questioned and challenged after they experience abuse, it's painful.

When someone is telling their story, the chances are that they are telling the truth are high. The likelihood that sexual abuse claims are falsified has been found to be between 2 and 10 percent (at most). That means when someone is coming forward with their story, there's at the very least a 90 percent chance they are telling the truth.[14]

And that's just when in an individual case. In the case of several reports, the likelihood of truthfulness rises even more. As confusing as it can be when a leader is publicly accused of such crimes, it's best to keep skepticism to yourself and become prayer support for the process.

---

[14] David Lisak, Lori Gardinier, Sarah C Nicksa, and Ashley M Cote, "False allegations of sexual assault:
an analysis of ten years of reported cases," Violence Against Women no. 16 (December 2010):1318–34,
doi: 10.1177/1077801210387747.

If you have been falsely accused in the past, any accusations against someone you love and respect can be significantly triggering. I know the reality of this as well. Here are a few things to remember.

First, just because we love and respect someone does not mean that we can tie our experiences together. This is a hard pill to swallow, but just because you were falsely accused in the past doesn't mean every accusation against anyone else is false. Also, it doesn't mean it's true. At times, we truly just don't know, and our experiences and pain projections don't aid in the process of determining the truth of the situation. If you love a leader and accusations arise, I encourage you to come to the place of prayer so you can see the accusations for what they are and go to the section of this book that discusses trust. You may need to process some of this pain in a journal. In the privacy of your prayer relationship, cry out your thoughts. Here are some possible questions to ask as you process in prayer and journaling:

What if these accusations are true? How does

that affect my life?

What if these accusations are false? How does that affect my life?

Transformation

_____
_____
_____
_____
_____
_____
_____
_____
_____

Then, like the finale in the section on building trust with yourself, ask the Lord to reveal truth of your identity regardless of the outcome and write it out.

_____
_____
_____
_____
_____
_____
_____
_____
_____
_____
_____

_____
_____
_____
_____
_____

Whether the accusations are true or false, you can't do much as an outsider. Yes, you may feel a sense of responsibility to come to a personal conviction as to the truth of the situation, but really, you might be too close to make an authentic determination of truth. If you have been impacted by a ministry that is later accused of abuse, recognize your potential bias in the situation. Again, that is not a rubber stamp of guilty, but your bias should not be used to shame those in pain.

There are no winners in situations like this. No matter who is right or wrong in a situation, everyone involved walks away in pain. If the accusations do turn out to be false, those claims were created and designed by the enemy to destroy lives and leave marks. False accusations are also cultivated inside the hearts of struggling people who are suffering symptoms of mental illness themselves. Again, pain is present all the way around. Nevertheless, we must not contribute to these accusations out of our deficit to stir up pain and dissension. These impossible situations are invitations to connect with the peace of God and be a comfort to those around you as you feel the weight of pain and disappointment yourself. In time, God can break through even the toughest of situations like this.

GIVE AND TAKE RELATIONSHIPS

Relationship as defined by Oxford Languages is described as "the way in which two or more concepts, objects, or people are connected, or the state of being connected."[15] An even more interesting definition for Christians would be "the state of being connected by blood or marriage." Because of Jesus' sacrifice on the cross, we are connected in relationship. Scripture talks about the body of Christ as a body connected by his blood.

---

[15] Oxford Learner's Dictionaries, s.v. ("relationship," (n.)," accessed January 3, 2024, https://www.oxfordlearnersdictionaries.com/us/definition/english/relationship?q=relationship.

If you are a new Christian, this might feel like odd terminology. But in time and through discipleship, you will start to recognize the sacrifice of lambs in connection with Jesus's death on the cross as he represents a pure and spotless lamb.

> Just as a body, though one, has many parts, but all its many parts form one body, so it is with Christ. For we were all baptized by one Spirit so as to form one body— whether Jews or Gentiles, slave or free—and we were all given the one Spirit to drink. Even so the body is not made up of one part but of many. Now if the foot should say, "Because I am not a hand, I do not belong to the body," it would not for that reason stop being part of the body. And if the ear should say, "Because I am not an eye, I do not belong to the body," it would not for that reason stop being part of the body. If the whole body were an eye, where would the sense of hearing be? If the whole body were

> an ear, where would the sense of smell be? But in fact God has placed the parts in the body, every one of them, just as he wanted them to be. If they were all one part, where would the body be? As it is, there are many parts, but one body."
> (1 Corinthians 12:12–20 NIV)

Because of the sacrifice of Jesus on the cross, we have the ability to live as God's very children. We aren't distant relatives but one body. We all serve different parts of the body with different giftings. When the Bible talks about one part of the body not needing another, this directly correlates to pain from others in community. We can come to the place where we determine that we don't need each other. This is goes against our very own faith. We need each other. What's more is we don't just need a tiny clique or a best friend in the church to meet our own needs. We need multiple reciprocal relationships of all different kinds. We shouldn't be friends only with the eyes of the body and not feet. (I sometimes inevitably equate these roles of eyes and feet to seers and missionary evangelists.)

We all have a specific calling. As we grow in that calling, we may wrongly think that everyone else should be focused on that calling too. When Rob and I were young missionaries, we had a hard time wondering why anyone would want to pastor a church in America. Yes, I'm exposing our own immaturity years ago. We thought everyone should be as zealous for the mission field as we were. Since then, the Lord has shown us in that others have different gifts and are called to different ministries within the body of Christ.

The same is true within relationships. One of the most complex concepts to learn about give and take within relationships is that you will have differences in what each person offers and accepts in each relationship. So learn where you are gifted and where others are gifted. Some people are truly empathetic and can be by your side in a hard time. These people might give hours of their time to process difficulties alongside you but may struggle to keep up with organization in their home. If you offer them a gift of an acts of service as their love language, you may want to come over their house occasionally and help them restructure. We all give and take in different ways, and we can learn to do this in a lot of beautiful ways.

Dive into books specifically for the purpose of relationship building so that you can learn how to set and maintain boundaries and learn what and how to contribute to relationships in a healthy way.

When someone has lost trust in the dynamic of community after being hurt, they may struggle to maintain the trust necessary for employing these behaviors. Just like in previous sections with trust, when it comes to our relationship with God and our relationship with self, we must come to a place of vulnerability where we can process the way our pain has interfered with our trust for others.

In the same way we processed our self-protection mechanisms that were birthed from toxic beliefs about ourselves, we will now do this in relation to community. What are the ugly truths about people that are being fed by traumatic historical events in your life?

_____
_____
_____
_____
_____
_____
_____
_____
_____
_____
_____
_____
_____
_____
_____
_____
_____

I will reiterate what I recommended the last time we did this.

Once you finish the above activity, put this book down, and feel the feelings. Put worship on, punch a pillow, scream, scribble, rip up paper or tissues, cry, and turn up the worship music even louder. Do not pretend to control this process. You are in process right now as you read these words. The more you allow yourself to feel and embrace the expression of your emotions, the more successful your process will be. Do this until you start to calm down and feel waves of relief. At that point, you may be tired and need to rest. The Lord may also reveal truth to you about your identity or how he feels about you. Write them in the section below or in your journal.

The purpose for this part of the process is that you will never be able to build a sense of trust in relationship with others until you vulnerably assess the pre-existing pain caused by the traumas. Now, like in the section before, I can list tons of passages on community that you can pray and meditate on, but again, you can Google and look up those passages that best apply to you. What many battle in relationship can be traced back to abusive behavior or neglect from another, which can cause a fear of abandonment. Fear of abandonment can become an extreme problem for some that really drives insecure behavior and attachment to others. Now we need attachment to people in the context of relationship and community, but when this need is driven by fears from our traumatic history, we leave room for error in how we interpret and behave in relationships.

The underlying fears concerning abandonment and abuse should be processed in the journal, and just like before, bring the journal entries to therapy or inner healing if you incorporate these services into your healing process.

REBUILDING TRUST IN RELATIONSHIP WITH OTHERS

I'm not merely discussing rebuilding trust after a broken relationship with other people. Sometimes, we get to the place of brokenness in relationship that we actually lose faith in the ability to re-establish relationships. We create our own sense of safety in isolation and start to believe the lie that we will be okay alone. Of course, in time, we learn that we aren't actually okay alone. At the same time, we may need a time of recovery after trauma and limit contact with others. This is normal. When we are sick, we need to take time to rest and recover. The same thing is true when we are suffering after trauma or struggle with symptoms of mental illness.

WITHDRAWAL AND ISOLATION

At times in Scripture, even Jesus drew away to process with the Lord. He had a few disciples in proximity, but he spent time with the Lord alone in Gethsemane. He was under such great stress that he sweat drops of blood as he prayed.

He was up against some of the worst betrayal he would face yet, including the infamous denial of relationship by Peter and the selling of his very life by his once disciple Judas. If anyone understands pain in community, it's Jesus. For this reason, we should follow His example and slip away from society for a time to process, pray, and heal for a time. The emphasis here is on the limited amount of time. This season should not span years. If you take too long, you run the risk of isolating yourself. The relationship skills you once had may grow dull, and trauma will define your interactions.

As you process, you may need to repeat some steps, depending on the depth of the impact. In this next section, start writing what God has said over your relationships and about who you are in the midst of them. The resistance here may be words you were cursed with during past relationship conflicts. Sometimes when relationships go south, people verbally attack and gossip, which can do significant damage. In order to process the truth of who you are in the context of relationships, you may need to write the exact opposite of what was said to find the truth. Don't regurgitate a bunch of verses here, though you should be able to confirm your identity with the Bible. Now, close your eyes and block out the world around you.

Ask God genuinely and sincerely, "What is the *actual* truth about your desire for me to thrive in relationship and my identity in the context of relationship?"

_____
_____
_____
_____
_____
_____
_____
_____
_____
_____
_____
_____
_____
_____
_____
_____
_____
_____
_____

One of the most important transitions in this process will be reintegration into community. As you look for a safe community to integrate into, you will need to refer to previous sections of this book that discuss what a healthy community looks like and what safe leadership looks like. This may be challenging because we can be a little blind to areas that have contributed negatively to our relationships. When we have problems in relationships, we may struggle to believe we can succeed in this area.

HOW TRAUMA IMPACTS RELATIONSHIPS

There's a difference between withdrawing to pray and recover from social life and isolating. This is especially true if you are wired to measure the physical energy of social interactions. When you withdraw in a healthy way, it empowers you to go out again. We are designed for connection and attachment. Even if social interactions seem to take a lot out of you, you are still created to have those experiences.

Sometimes people are unaware of their isolation tendencies. This can be tough, especially when you are going through seasons of hardship. One way to know if you are starting to isolate is if it starts to feel impossible to go out and engage in normal activities with others. Withdrawing for a time is healthy and productive, but long-term isolation is potentially dangerous and symptomatic.

You see, the very definition of isolation means to cut off relationship. This term is also used in connection with severe illness. Someone who is isolating over the long-term might be really suffering and struggling. If you find that you are doing this, don't wait to reach out for help. At times when I was dealing with a situation, I wasn't sure if it was bad compared to what others were facing. I thought I should keep silent and figure it out on my own. But that thought process breeds the cycle of isolation. It's rooted in feeling as if your experiences aren't real or valid and also in a poor self-image.

Here's the scale I would use to determine if

you should reach out for help. If you don't think you need help, you might not need any help. If you think you need help, you should absolutely reach out for help. If you are unsure if your issues or experiences are bad enough to see help, if that is even a question in your mind, I'll give you a very simple answer: Yes, you need help. You might not need extensive help, but if you have a fleeting thought that "I might need help," then do not hesitate to ask for it. Reach out to a friend, pastor, or counselor for some added support. Are you in crisis? Maybe not. But avoiding that subtle thought of "I need help" is the step right before crisis. It hardly ever improves from there without a miracle. We can be so hard on ourselves too. We can question our own motives for reaching out. "What if they think I'm doing this for attention?"

Can I tell you a secret? It's *okay*. You probably aren't doing it for attention if you are asking that question. Even so, if you do need attention, that's okay too.

When I became a parent, I was having a really hard time. We traveled a lot, and I truly had no idea how to parent at all. My children weren't always behaving to standards of others who were critical, and I did not receive much encouragement. I was really hard on myself and was told I was a bad parent. The harder I was on my son and the more I demanded his obedience, the more defiant he became. At the same time, people in the church told me I needed to learn how to parent. (Ironically, people often compliment me on my children now, but hopefully, this story gets a point across.)

My son started to refuse to clean up his toys and said, "No, Mommy." I became so strict on him, not believing a word he would tell me. I was so conditioned to believe that I was a bad parent and that my child was not listening to me. I just wanted him to be obedient like a "good" child. I became so angry at times, and I would soon regret it.

One day, we ran into a couple from church. My son was acting up again. He complained of feeling sick to his stomach, but I struggled to believe him. I had no good counsel for parenting. The friend from church looked at my son holding his belly and said, "Oh, my kids do this all the time. They are doing it for attention." I became angry yet again. My son was acting out for attention, and even others could see it. I prayed to God for a connection with my son because nothing I said or did seemed to make him just obey. I mean, he was four years old and just acting out.

Less than a week later, my son was in the hospital connected to tubes and on the verge of death. He had been telling me that he was tired and couldn't pick up his toys because he had a stomachache. He wasn't seeking attention even though it seemed like that to everyone else. I felt like a failure. He was crying out for help, and I was punishing him. He had numerous bruises on his legs, not because he was a boy but due to low platelets. He was diagnosed with high-risk acute lymphoblastic leukemia B-cell, treatable with an 80 percent success rate for the next five years and 3.5 years of intensive treatment that included blood transfusions, all kinds of chemo, port placement, injections, spinal taps, and more. This was one of the absolute worst experiences of our lives. I wish I had the revelation of people needing attention that I do now.

You should talk about what you are going through, and as a coach in grad school who plans to become a therapist in the future, it is a leader's responsibility to help you learn boundaries. Even the need for attention is symptomatic of needing connection because you have a deficit. This need could point to serious struggle that won't get better until you get the courage to *speak it*. So in a helping relationship with a healthy leader, they will be able to handle it if you struggle with appropriate boundaries. You don't need to be embarrassed about that. Reach out to healthy friends and community or reputable ministers or therapists.

And to boot, everyone needs attention, and it's okay to reach out for that too. Do you hear me? Reach out for attention before isolation. Connect in. Attach to people even if you don't know all the right ways too. Look for the healthy ones who can assert their boundaries, and you will learn but you will also get that love and belonging cup filled. Have grace for your mistakes and educate yourself where you can. Danny Silk and Dr. Henry Cloud have some great resources on keeping love on in community, boundaries, safe people and more. I highly recommend their resources.

At the end of the day, don't confuse withdrawing for strength, prayer and recovery with isolating that leads to sickness and potentially worse. Attention is a normal need so even if you fear that may be your burden, connect to other healthy individuals, and it will work out in the end if you are receptive to how others set boundaries. If you fear you are isolating, reach out for help.

WHAT IS HELP?

"I lift up my eyes to the mountains— where does my help come from? My help comes from the Lord, the Maker of heaven and earth. He will not let your foot slip—he who watches over you will not slumber" (Psalm 121:1–3).

Scripture talks about the Lord being our help and providing our help. In this context, I believe that the things that truly help us are from Him. I believe He uses a lot of different things to help us. This is not to say that everything we think helps us is actually helping us. When I was seventeen years old, I dropped out of college to enter a life of intensive therapies. I was very blessed with a year of dialectical behavioral therapy, which if you didn't know, is an intensive treatment for borderline personality disorder that I was diagnosed with. BPD is very hard to live with and recover from, but DBT has very high success rates with those who are motivated to work at it. I say this because when I recount my testimony of coming through years of intensive treatment and mental health disorders, I talk about how God set me free from a life of dysfunction with mental health disorders. I was even deemed by the government incompetent to function in society and qualified for all kinds of help to survive. After I experienced healing from the Lord, I rejected the help from the government. This is no shame to those who need it and it helped me during the seasons I was in treatment. I wanted to work really hard in my life and I didn't want any shortcuts if at all possible. Now there were times before that point that those supports kept me alive and I'm always thankful. I did not think I was truly incompetent though. I was ready to soar, and I did, all glory to Jesus Christ.

At the same time, when I recount my testimony, I do not claim to be delivered from the treatments. No, I believe that was all part of the "help" that comes from the Lord like that in Psalm 121:1-3. He doesn't provide help defined by our terms. He provides help based on our need. He knows what we need. After we went through the exposure of the abusive ministry I referenced in the beginning of this book, I returned for a season of professional counseling with a Christian counselor and I also worked through my own Mashah Inner Healing sessions. You see? Therapy, inner healing and services like that are not the enemy you need to be delivered from. They are part of your deliverance from the pain and trauma you endured. God uses all of them.

I state this because there are people in the Church who believe therapy is not of God. How very sad to have this perspective. I'm not saying it's the be all end all or that it always works out how we're hoping. I've had less than stellar experiences in counseling throughout my life. You need to find a good counselor you can build rapport with. If you don't click with the counselor you find, that's okay.

So what is help? Helps is whatever the Lord leads you to make it to the next step in your journey. When I work with people and they are really struggling, sometimes I notice that they are fearing 5 and 10 years down the road. When you are going through some rough stuff, you do not need to worry about what life will be like 10 years down the road or next week. You just have to make it through today in the Lord. You have to just think about your next meal and your next step. Don't fear tomorrow, as tomorrow has troubles of its own. (See Matthew 6:34.)

It's normal to want to look ahead, but when we do it out of fear, we will not get a true scope of what that will look like anyway. So if you are battling fear of the future, embrace today with the Lord. Just think about the next step he leads you to. And if he leads you to professional counseling, then that's the help he's providing. If he leads you to Mashah Inner Healing and Deliverance, then that's the help he's providing. We don't have to have it all figured out, just ask him for the next step. That is your help. It may even be a call to a friend. That, my friend, is your help.

THE INTERPERSONAL IMPACTS OF TRAUMA

We've already talked about how skewed things may be when coming from traumatic experiences and trying to rebuild the relationships in your life. I can speak from the perspective of having battled borderline personality disorder as an example. When I was diagnosed with it as a young person, it was highly stigmatized. However, years later, the diagnosis is more common. It's still highly stigmatized but a little less. It's a good example of how trauma can impact your relationships.

BPD is known to be likely caused from abuse and neglect in childhood, which was definitely present in mine. One of the things people with BPD can do is called "splitting" and it's really hard to describe if you've never experienced it. It's like a phenomenon where you are on good terms with someone, and then someone says something that subconsciously reminds you of a time that you were damaged. You aren't cognitive that it's happening without therapy and awareness. All you get is an emotional flashback where you are feeling with that person in that moment the same way that you felt in an abusive situation. The emotion triggers your response as if the person you are with was your abuser. From the outside perspective, it looks like you were happy with the person one moment and then you suddenly flip a switch to anger. It's a hard concept to grasp because when you do it, you aren't even aware of it.

Eventually, if you keep responding in this way with people, you will not be able to handle close relationships very easily. You may even gain a reputation for being manipulative or unstable. People will back off from you in fear that you are unsafe, but from your perspective, you will truly be confused. If you relate to these experiences, run, don't walk to therapy. God uses it to help the abused. You don't deserve that switch in your brain that causes such confusion, and I promise you that there are trustworthy people who will not abuse you, but until you work through some of your pain at the deepest levels, you'll always confuse the good people with the bad ones. Some of these issues simply cannot be addressed in a book, and you will need to reach out for help. God can and will heal you. He will use these professional resources to change our lives like he did mine. I wasn't delivered from therapy; God used therapy to deliver me from the parts of myself that would have destroyed me if I didn't trust him with the process. Therapy is a tool God uses for his people.

For some, professional help when they are suffering is truly hard to get into. There is a shortage of help in certain areas, and waitlists can be long. Insurance might not cover therapy, but you can still take certain steps. Look for help on a sliding scale fee or purchase a cheap workbook on Amazon. Sometimes churches have healthy trained leadership that can help people who are going through hard times. Look into addiction support groups because addiction often accompanies isolation. These groups are usually free. The hardest step will be reaching out the first time and going to therapy or a group meeting. Once you do it, you will be able to go again.

As you actively seek support for any extreme thoughts or struggles you may have, try to find safe places to connect. Many experts now believe addiction is actually an attachment disorder.[16] Many develop these issues because their need for attachment has been denied, and then they continue to deny themselves the very attachment they need. You shouldn't be punished for this, but pick yourself up and get into community somewhere, someway. It's not easy but it's worth it.

---

[16] Andreas Schindler, "Attachment and Substance Use Disorders—Theoretical Models, Empirical Evidence, and Implications for Treatment," Front Psychiatry, no. 10 (October 2019):727, doi: 10.3389/fpsyt.2019.00727.

Rebuilding trust in relationships takes courage. You can't quit the moment things go wrong. You can't give up when it gets hard. You have to be open to the idea that trauma affects your perception. You have to be open to seeing things less black and white and more gray.

Read, research, use trial and error, and learn what you can about community. As someone who has experienced more social struggles than many, I relate to how hard this can be. People expect you to not be traumatized in community. People expect you to catch the social cues. People don't understand dissociation or flashbacks. I understand every single aspect of this, along with possibly becoming an outcast if you let your guard down. But if you keep trying, you will find your people, I promise. Try to have grace for those who don't understand even when you need grace yourself. Forgive and move forward with love.

PRAISE THROUGH SUDDEN DEVASTATION

One of the most common feelings people face after they've been through serious trauma is abandonment. They have a deep reverence for God, but they have trouble feeling him through the pain of what they are experiencing. When my son was going through cancer treatments at four years old, I had a lot of questions for God. I didn't feel my family deserved this. We were (and are) a God-fearing ministry family who prayed our kids into existence even through the curse of barrenness. We served the Lord with all our hearts, souls, and minds. So needless to say, when we were hit with the shock of his diagnosis, we understandably had a lot of questions.

And you know what? God can handle our questions. Our ideas of our Everlasting Father are too fragile. A good father gives good gifts to his children. If those gifts are answers, he has them for you. Sometimes we don't receive those answers until heaven, but he has answers for us and is near even in the time of our questioning.

At times, I struggled to feel the Lord even after years of ministry. In the middle of the night, the machines were beeping from my son's monitors, and I cried out to the Lord silently, "Why?" I wondered if my brokenness might be too ugly for him or repel him in some way. But the truth is the exact opposite. The Bible says this: "The Lord is near to the brokenhearted and saves the crushed in spirit" (Psalm 34:18 ESV).

Actually, brokenness doesn't repel God; in fact, he draws near to it. He draws near to us! Another powerful passage that God led me to refers to our weakness as a catalyst for his strength.

> Three times I pleaded with the Lord about this, that it should leave me. But he said to me, "My grace is sufficient for you, for my power is made perfect in weakness." Therefore I will boast all the more gladly of my weaknesses, so that the power of Christ may rest upon me. For the sake of Christ, then, I am content with weaknesses, insults, hardships, persecutions, and

> calamities. For when I am weak, then I am strong. (2 Corinthians 12:8–10 ESV)

This revelation was especially powerful to me in times of deep hardship. If you've read this passage before but have since been through traumatic experiences, read it again in light of your current circumstances. As the younger generations would say, it hits different. When you go through painful situations, you can feel unreasonably weak. Sometimes people have trouble even getting out of bed. They become so fatigued and can't complete normal tasks. At the end of the day, it's okay to be weak. It's okay to go through hard seasons because it is an opportunity for God to show himself powerful in and through your life.

Many think that the trick in Christianity is not showing weakness. If we paint on our smiles and show up, then we are handling life. We become experts at suppressing how we really feel and struggling alone. The truth is, weakness allows for the power of God to be made perfect and sufficient through us when we allow for openness and vulnerability. It takes a deep level of strength in order to function in the strength of the Lord amidst our own weakness.

With those two passages alone, we can combat a lot of feelings that arise from the flesh in hard times. We can address the invitation to conformity. We can be honest when we feel that he is not close in our brokenness or when we feel too weak to move on. The truth of the matter is that he is especially close in those broken seasons and our weakness is the very prerequisite for his strength being made perfect in our lives. If we could do it in our own power, what would that say about our need for his strength? If we were unworthy because of our weakness, what would it say about his strength? The answers to those questions are that we are not tirelessly strong and his strength is sufficient in our weakness. This is all the more reason to praise; because when we feel we can't, the Holy Spirit in us can.

We talked about how trauma is an interruption throughout this book. We've also talked a bit about how healing is an interruption. Healing is a powerful interruption that can penetrate the depths of bondage that comes after being hit by traumas. Even if you've chosen the road of conforming to the patterns of the world, there's never a moment that you can't turn your pain into desperate praise.

Healing is a disruption to abusive and destructive patterns. Abuse doesn't stop with the experience itself. Abuse continues and turns into self-abuse when we turn to the patterns of the world. This is the danger of going through traumatic illnesses like post-traumatic stress disorders, personality disorders, depressive disorders, and more because trauma can develop patterns of self-abuse that set a person on a trajectory of pain that progressively worsens. This is also why, throughout this book, I've discussed the very seriousness of addressing issues as soon as possible. It's easier to stand up from a chair than the floor. If we can catch some of these patterns while you are sitting in the chair, you may have the strength to stand up before you fall on the floor.

When someone falls to the floor, they may need help to get off the floor. Various factors affect this: cause of injury, loss of strength, their age, etc. If someone is seventy-three years old and suffers from certain conditions, a fall can be fatal. If someone is twenty-two and falls but suffers from early onset osteoporosis, they may need the same level of help the seventy-three-year-old would need when they fall. This might seem like an extreme example but it does happen, and one of my own siblings had early onset osteoporosis.

People would look at my family member and think that it was impossible that they suffered from bone troubles or that maybe his struggles were to get attention. We've already been over that topic. We cannot control how others perceive our attempts at recovery, but be encouraged that reaching out for help is a courageous step. You already know you may get different reactions when you do, but move beyond the fear of others and take practical action.

When people don't physically see the struggle, such as with invisible PTSD and invisible early onset osteoporosis, they may be skeptical. But at some point, they will go through experiences themselves that help validate your perspective and grow their sense of empathy. You may not have the time to wait for them to mature in this way, so please don't.

As I previously stated, renewal is the very process of restarting after an interruption.[17] So when we are talking about healing, we are talking about interrupting negative processes and seeing fruitful positive outcomes that lead to the trajectory of new creation reality, life, and fulfillment. This has both practical and spiritual aspects. Be sure to take practical steps while you engage with the supernatural for your healing.

One of the first steps you can take is found in the foundational Scripture of this book. "Be transformed by the renewing of your mind." However, you cannot do this while you are conforming to the patterns of the world.

---

[17] Oxford's Learner's Dictionary, "renewal."

In order to be transformed, you must renounce and reject any conformity to the world. This means if you are drinking to cope, you must stop. If you are self-injuring, you must stop. If you are maintaining lifestyles of various sexual addictions, you must stop. If you are manipulating or abusing others, you must stop. However, when this involves others, you must find a trusted person to hold you accountable for your past aggressions and keep you from continuing them.

Some may feel they cannot stop. I agree: You cannot stop conforming to the world, at least in your own power. You must simultaneously reject conformity at the same time you are embracing transformation. One of the ways I recommend doing this is through praise.

POWER OF PRAISE

Music holds power, and I used to use some horrible music to fuel my pain and aggression in my teenage years. Not only was I a self-injurer, but I was always looking for music that heightened the emotions as I self-destructed. Some of the artists I listened to were unhealed themselves, meditating and chanting the worst possible lyrics of aggression and pain. When I started to embrace transformation, I embraced a new lifestyle with it.

Oh, how I hear the painful moans of people who think I'm being religious when I share this. I can say that you may not have the conviction to listen to only Christian music, but that's off topic from what I'm addressing right now. However, when you've been through traumas, be aware that the pain in your soul will connect with the pain in other souls, even through their art. Either your pain will connect in a way that fuels the depth of pain and conformity to the patterns of the world, or your pain will be healed and you will connect to others' pain in a way that lifts them from drowning. This isn't a call for you to be a hero, but inevitably it will become a part of your life, a tool God uses to reach others.

Even if you don't have a conviction to listen to only Christian music, I do propose that in the seasons where you need deep healing, you play worship and praise music nearly constantly. In this time, alongside whatever help services God provides you to work through your past or current issues, maintain an atmosphere of worship and praise. You do not have to have the energy to even sing. If you are allowed to wear headphones where you work, turn the music on low. Play praise and worship in your car as you travel. Fight the urge to feed your depression with darkness. Just releasing praise and worship in the atmosphere can make all the difference in how much the pain takes control of your life. Praise and worship conditions our minds and hearts for the awareness of his presence. We become keep in our spiritual object permanence.

There are countless peer-reviewed studies to show that when people listen to gospel music, for example, the associations of death and anxiety decreased and a sense of control in the person's life increased. These results were the same despite demographics, socioeconomic states, gender, or other variables.[18] Now I personally like more contemporary worship, but most theologically sound worship and praise will have this effect. This is not

bondage. You're not playing praise and worship because you are craving music.
No, I'm prescribing praise and worship as a lifestyle. Listen when you sleep, too, if possible. Listen when the pain is great. Listen when you cry alone. Listen when life is unbearable and when life is great. It is step one in your treatment plan.

Step two is working through this book as many times as you need to. Some of the self-processing in select chapters may need to be revisited and journaled out again and again. Step three is reaching out as the Holy Spirit leads you to start talking about what you've been through.

Transformation by the renewing of the mind is not a temporary good feeling. It's a new way of life. Sometimes we allow the Lord to bring us to the point where we are feeling okay for a moment.

---

[18] Matt Bradshaw, Christopher G Ellison, Qijuan Fang, and Collin Mueller, "Listening to Religious Music
and Mental Health in Later Life," Gerontologist, no. 55 (December 2015):961–71, doi: 10.1093/geront/gnu020.

If the pain continues in waves, start processing in accountable ways with others as has been mentioned. Again, I can't say this enough: Therapy and inner healing are great ways to do this.

To recap some of the main points in this book, here is your treatment plan.

Name:_____

Date: _____

Diagnosis: No weapon formed against you shall prosper. (Isaiah 54:17)

Treatment plan:
• Reject previous and current patterns of conformity to patterns of the world.

• Receive transformation by the renewing of the mind, praise, worship and the Word of God.

• Become willing to receive help and become proactive by following the leading of the Lord to invest in and engage in helpful services from an objective perspective, which will allow an outside party to speak into your struggles.

• Be accountable and truthful in ways that might even be uncomfortable. (Who am I kidding? It absolutely will be uncomfortable and may even make you feel like jumping out of your skin, but it's the only way forward.)

• Be committed to battling fleshy forms of self-protection that lead to covert self-destruction in the process.

• Talk about the hardest topics in the safest settings.

• If you lapse in progress, get back up where you left off. Don't stay stuck. Keep moving forward.

GOOD PEOPLE *DO* RECOVER

In the midst of devastation, you may find it hard to believe that good people do recover.

Especially in the cases of narcissistic abuse, you might wonder if it was worth it to say anything at all about your experiences. You may see people you believe are not good succeed. (At least from your perspective, they are not good.) This passage is so encouraging as well. I have highlighted just a few verses, but the whole chapter covers this topic.

> Hope in the Lord and keep his way. He will exalt you to inherit the land; when the wicked are destroyed, you will see it. I have seen a wicked and ruthless man flourishing like a luxuriant native tree, but he soon passed away and was no more; though I looked for him, he could not be found.
>
> Consider the blameless, observe the upright; a future awaits those who seek peace. But all sinners will be destroyed; there will be no future for the wicked. (Psalm 37:34–38 NIV)

When cases of abuse come forward, one of the knee jerk reactions of society is to turn on the victim of the abuse. This does not give credibility to the counter-accusations or the reality of your experience.

God doesn't lie. Scripture talks about everything that is done and said in darkness coming to light.

> The time is coming when everything that is covered up will be revealed, and all that is secret will be made known to all. Whatever you have said in the dark will be heard in the light, and what you have whispered behind closed doors will be shouted from the housetops for all to hear! Dear friends, don't be afraid of those who want to kill your body; they cannot do any more to you after that. (Luke 12:2-4)

You see, in the end, you may have to process some of the worst pain when seems like the bad guys get away with doing wrong. It feels like a violation when you've done everything right and don't feel as if you can get closure. If you are in that situation, God has seen it all. Everything that is covered up will be revealed. All the hidden secrets will be made known to *all*. I love that it says *all* right there in that verse because even God sees fit to vindicate you in your testimony.

People in abusive relationships will take the Bible out of context to trap you. One example of this is when people use the verse, "Love covers a multitude of sins" (1 Peter 4:8). The context here is refraining from undue gossip and humiliation about someone's struggles in an effort to show genuine and deep love for one another. This is the opposite of what people do in abusive situations.

When we refer back to the passage in Luke 12:2-4, we can see that those who use 1 Peter 4:8 out of context will be exposed for the ways they continue to hurt people. In the right heart and mind, we pray they are exposed in a way that leads to their genuine repentance. Another great reference for this is Ecclesiastes 12:14: "For God shall bring every work into judgment, with every secret thing, whether it be good, or whether it be evil" (KJV).

You can trust God: Nobody will get away with anything. At the same time, he doesn't allow us to partake in vengeance because we are not designed for it. This is where the power of forgiveness comes into play.

POWER OF FORGIVENESS

When people are hurt at deep levels, we can experience emotions that fuel negative behaviors. We may be tempted to take aggressive action toward others while we struggle within ourselves.

> Let love be without hypocrisy. Abhor what is evil. Cling to what is good. Be kindly affectionate to one another with brotherly love, in honor giving preference to one another; not lagging in diligence, fervent in spirit, serving the Lord; rejoicing in hope, patient in tribulation, continuing steadfastly in

prayer; distributing to the needs of the saints, given to hospitality.

Bless those who persecute you; bless and do not curse. Rejoice with those who rejoice, and weep with those who weep. Be of the same mind toward one another. Do not set your mind on high things, but associate with the humble. Do not be wise in your own opinion.

Repay no one evil for evil. Have regard for good things in the sight of all men. If it is possible, as much as depends on you, live peaceably with all men. Beloved, do not avenge yourselves, but rather give place to wrath; for it is written, "Vengeance is Mine, I will repay," says the Lord. Therefore

"If your enemy is hungry, feed him;

If he is thirsty, give him a drink;

For in so doing you will heap coals

of fire on his head."

> Do not be overcome by evil, but overcome evil with good. (Romans 12:9–21)

This Scripture doesn't soothe your flesh or allow you to act out in pain. It takes a true transformative mindset to be able to function in this level of forgiveness and blessing, but notice the first part of the passage. It speaks on love being opposite of hypocrisy. When we take vengeance into our own hands, we risk becoming hypocrites and stepping out of the reality of love. The danger of hypocrisy is that it makes us like the very people who hurt us.

Hypocrisy turns us into our abusers. It's becoming more common knowledge that people who abuse others are often products of abuse themselves. Did you ever wonder why? This is not a pass at empathy that enables abuse. Many people confuse that as well. But the more we recognize these patterns, the more we can come to the understanding of the role we play if we conform to the patterns of the world through hypocrisy.

Statistics show that more than half (51 percent) of people who have gone through abuse as children would go onto experience domestic abuse in their adult years and, in turn, suffer higher rates of mood/personality disorders, addiction, and disability.[19] People who commit crimes against children are disordered 100 percent of the time. This is my own statistic because in order to harm a child, a person must have a disordered mindset that is birthed out of dysfunction in a person's life. From this, we can conclude that experiencing disordered perspectives leaves us vulnerable to a higher risk of becoming like those who hurt us.

You may think, *I would never do the things that were done to me*. And that may very well be true. But would you pass on the mindsets that would do as much damage to your own children because you refuse to do the work to face how the disordered pain has affected your own life? As harsh as that sounds, it's very destructive. We must choose transformation by the renewing of our mind so we can know what is good and what the will of God is for our lives. Disorder leaves us conforming to a confused state of what is good and bad.

Transformation

Transformation leaves us renewed in a new creation reality with the mind of Christ that can forgive and be accountable to what is good.

I say this because you've probably heard about the importance of forgiveness and how it works a million times. Forgiveness sets the victim free to no longer live as a victim. Forgiveness does not okay the offensive and abusive behavior, and we already know that God takes care of those. We do not have to take vengeance ourselves. Vengeance is his! What's equally important in understanding the power of forgiveness is realizing the dangers if we choose not to forgive.

I've heard some perspectives on forgiveness contrary to this message, and I truly examined them

---

[19] "People who were abused as children are more likely to be abused as an adult," Office for National
Statistics, September 27, 2017,
https://www.ons.gov.uk/peoplepopulationandcommunity/crimeandjustice/articles/peoplewhowereabuseda
schildrenaremorelikelytobeabusedasanadult/2017-09-27.

But ultimately, when we harbor unforgiveness (after we have had time to process, pray, and heal), we run the risk of reaping all the deficits that left our abuser with the mindset that empowered them to hurt us.

So forgiveness is more than important—it's vital. After we process the harm that has been done to us, we must come to the place that we chose to forgive and move on, remembering God uses both time and process as tools for our healing. We may remember the events and the lessons that impacted us, but we don't keep replaying them to decide if and how we will engage in community in the future. This does not mean that we ignore red flags if we see them in the future. Absolutely not! You have wisdom and discernment you didn't have before, and not only will you be more aware of red flags, but God will use those lessons to help others if you allow him to.

Make a list of the people you need to forgive:

_____
_____
_____
_____

Transformation

_____
_____
_____
_____
_____
_____
_____
_____
_____
_____

Next, forgive them in prayer with your Heavenly Father as your witness.

Lord, I forgive _____ for _____, and I ask you to heal my heart from any damage they have caused me. I ask, God, that you put a stop to their patterns that they would have a complete turnaround. I pray for their repentance and salvation. I ask, God, that you heal me from the ways I've developed unhealthy patterns myself as a result of their behaviors and words against me. I think you, Lord, that you have a plan for my life. This is the beginning and not the end. I chose transformation by the renewing of my mind and not conformity to the patterns of this world. I release the offenders from my life, and I no longer allow them to impact my attachment to others. I will run toward healing, wholeness, the mind of Christ, resources you lead me to, community, and fearless risk in relationship once again. In Jesus's name. Amen.

Once you have walked in forgiveness, you now have a renewed mindset. Continue renewing your mindset through praise and worship, reading the Bible, fellowship with Christians, and growing in any areas of character and spiritual gifts you may need to. You are free from the shackles that once tried to entangle you, and though you may have fallen victim to sin against your will, you are no longer a victim. You are a victor.

LIVING A VICTORIOUS LIFE

So what does it mean to be a victor? It means that the process of healing now becomes empowering. You are no longer seeking help because you are drowning. You are owning your deficits and the areas of improvement in your life. You are building healthy relationships in your community and fearlessly diving in, serving in the community, fulfilling God-given roles as a child, parent, spouse, sibling, etc. You no longer identify with labels that tear you down.

Even if you have been diagnosed with labels that helped you get insurance for treatment or helped you understand how serious your issue was, these terms do not define your life, and you do not have to tack them onto your identity. You are a child of God, his beloved child. You are a new creation in Christ Jesus. You are healed, called, and anointed. This is the beginning and not the end. If you think you've already come a long way, you haven't seen anything yet.

Our words have power. We know this by verses like Proverbs 18:21. "Death and life are in the power of the tongue, and those who love it and indulge it will eat its fruit and bear the consequences of their words" (AMP).

When our son was diagnosed with cancer, we

had already asked all our friends and partners online to pray because we didn't actually know what was going on for a full twenty-four hours. They were running tests to let us know exactly what kind of cancer he would have, and we would have to decide how to proceed from there.

When we realized that the process would be years long, we had to decide what we would tell people and how we would process it. We went on Facebook and looked at other family's pages and how they presented going through cancer treatments to get ideas of this new world we were entering.

We found lots of ideas from great pages like "pray for this person" and "hope for that one." We decided early on that we weren't going to present this as a battle we were warring in but as a victory that had already been won on the cross. On the first day, when we announced our next steps and asked for prayers on the journey, we named our son's page Victory for Titus and used the same hashtag. Every time someone refer to what our son was going through, they had to acknowledge the victory.

This very practice was empowering, and we could feel the power in our words during this season. Our son didn't choose cancer at four years old or to have years of his life spent in intensive treatment. As parents, we would have done nearly anything to avoid this, but unfortunately, we couldn't. We couldn't avoid being targets of the weapon, but we knew the weapon wouldn't prosper.

In this same way, when some unforeseen attack hits you, you may fall victim to it for a minute. But you can speak victory into and over your situation. Name what you are going through "Victory over this" or "Victory for that." Living as a victor means thinking, talking, and behaving like a victor. It starts with the framework of speaking victory into who you are and over your situation.

CONCLUSION

In this book, we've covered topics that can transform your post-traumatic stress disorder and other related symptoms to praising through sudden devastation when you put these practices into effect. By gaining a sense of spiritual object permanence, you can move to a mature understanding of the presence of God despite terrible struggles you may have walked through. We can see God in many ways speaking to us, offering healing and manifesting his presence in our lives. Just because we may ask him for a specific manifestation of his presence doesn't mean he isn't with us or close to us or doesn't care about us. The more open we remain to his presence in the way he desires to manifest in our lives based on what he knows we need, the more receptive we will be on our own healing journey.

We've talked about how trauma is an

Conclusion

interruption and so is healing. The word *renewal* means to restart after an interruption, so when we see the words "be transformed by the renewing of our mind," we can see how God has a plan for comeback after trauma. Trauma is not the end of the road for his people. We may not all be exempt from experiencing it, but God has a plan for when we do. When we chose conformity to the patterns of the world, we allow for maladaptive coping, addiction, relationship issues, behaviors, and mindsets that allow serious disordered thinking to take root in our lives. When we allow ourselves to be transformed by the renewing of our minds, God literally restarts our transformation as if after the interruption of trauma and resets it. God interrupts our trauma with his healing, which you will be able to see in hindsight. In and through transformation by the renewing of your mind, you will begin to understand what is good, pleasing, and the will of God in accordance with Romans 12:2 (the very theme of this book).

In understanding goodness and pleasantness through transformation, you will gain deeper discernment. Many go for years conforming to the patterns of the world and don't know why they struggle to discern the will of God. We must embrace this transformation to lead healthy and fulfilling lives after trauma. The moment we come to the fork in the road between conformity and transformation, we must make the choice to walk the road of transformation. If you are reading the words on this page, it's not too late even if you already chose the road of conformity. You can cut through the grass and do the work to get on the right road from here.

In order to do this, we must understand the importance of and have clarity on the subject of accountability. Accountability is for us in every good way. It has healing properties and God uses this tool to help us achieve healthy attachment in community. God wants us leading honest and free lives. Living accountable according to Scripture empowers us to do so, but in order to truly live this way, we must feel and actually be safe in community.

Addressing safety in community is no easy

Conclusion

task when scandals of church hurt and abuse are trending. Is there a way to tell if you are in a safe environment to remain accountable? Why, yes there is. The very Word of God is for our benefit. The Bible helps us discern on our transformation journey, and only a safe church can offer the accountability a community needs to thrive. So refer back to the verses listed in previous chapters to test what God might have for you so that you understand where you are looking to remain accountable.

Healthy community functions in systems just like families. Family Systems Theory in psychology helps us understand the very dynamics that protect health within families, meet basic needs for the individuals, and function to protect the health of the overall body. If the family system within the community is unhealthy, the roles played will protect what is unhealthy. If the family system within the community is healthy, the roles played will protect all that is healthy.

You will be able to tell by fruit. Sometimes even these assessments can lead us to believe we see fruit, but we feel a check in our spirit. Let me break condemnation off you as some will call you suspicious when this happens, but it's okay to ask the Holy Spirit about those instances and not ignore your genuine feelings when discerning. In this way, the Holy Spirit will lead you as to if you should commit to a community or not. In commitment, you will embark on other risky behaviors like authenticity, relationship building, communication, working through disagreements, and so forth. Step one in this process is allowing the Holy Spirit to lead you to the right place with the right people. If you've already found them, the next step might be letting your guard down in ways you haven't yet to become more authentic or work through healing in areas you've not wanted to face. Then, you can also be there for others.

In order to understand healthy community, we have to understand healthy leadership. Leaders who abuse people are not fallen brothers. There is a protocol and high standard for leadership that should be taken into consideration before someone accepts a leadership role within an organization. This

Conclusion

falls under living above reproach, and within that context are a number of standards that were outlined so that not only can we understand the expectations and count the cost before we enter leadership ourselves, but we can know what to expect from others. Many don't have access to or think about what leadership standards should be. I hope this book helps a clear understanding of the weight and responsibility of leadership. Once we understand biblical leadership standards, we can normalize maintaining the standard, which is my heart for coming generations. We need a growing, healthy, vibrant, and beautiful church.

Once we've addressed healthy standards for community and leadership so that we can start or continue our process of growth, we can address the road of transformation. To embrace the start of our journey in transformation, we must take a look at our trust. We evaluate our trust with God, our trust with ourselves, and our trust with others. First, we must examine how some of the ways we have been hurt has skewed our ability to trust. When we break these down and build new foundations of trust, we can start to map out faith risks so that we can rebuild our lives in healthy ways. Risks are essential to growth. That makes them no less risky, but once you heal from past violated boundaries, you may be empowered with a greater sense of discernment for the future.

In order to know what to believe for and how to adopt kingdom strategies in community and healing, you need to understand basic human needs, including foundational levels of physiological essentials, safety and security, love and belonging, and morality and creativity. Each level builds on the previous but if the needs from the previous level are not met, you may ignore the upper levels. For instance, people who struggle to pay their bills may struggle to find a sense of creativity because the pressures of not having their safety and security met may also impact their physiological needs. When people struggle with low income, they find it hard to be creative. Additionally, when someone is living physiological distress long enough, they may struggle to have a sense of morality and engage in illegal behaviors, such as stealing.

Conclusion

When you are hungry enough and you see bread in the store, the lines of morality can blur. This isn't an excuse for this behavior, but it can certainly help us understand the very basics of human nature. We need to understand our needs in the order of importance so what we can put perspective on how to give and take in relationships in healthy ways that respect both our boundaries and those of others.

Diving further into the issue of trust, we need to address hard questions, such as "Where was God when I was abused?" Many ask this question when they are going through painful experiences they struggle to understand. When we understand God's presence in our lives, this can impact our trust level with him. If we believe that God was standing powerless during our abuse, we can feel victimized all over again. But when we see where God truly was during the abuse—on the cross of Calvary—we realize that while he was present with us, the actions taken against us put him back on the painful, excruciating cross. In those moments, we grasp how deeply and empathetically he relates to our pain.

We discussed self-trust, which can be reflected through the lens of self-hatred. Many people who have been through traumatic circumstances struggle with self-hatred. Unfortunately, the seed of self-hatred can grow into a toxic plant. You cannot live with this and thrive. Before you can ever get to a place of trusting yourself, your decisions, and your discernment, you must deal with any self-hatred. When this rears its ugly head, return to the appropriate chapters and do the exercises as needed. You may want a more private way to process your thoughts or may consider gifting the book in the future. Instead of filling in the blank spaces, just grab a cheap composition notebook and write your answers there.

Lastly, in the trust category, once we establish our trust with the Lord and with ourselves, we can dive into trust within community. Again, if you need to return to some of the exercises in this section, feel free to so do so. In order to thrive in community, we need to be able to establish trust for and with others. It will (and should) take time, but this journey, as scary as it can be for those who have been betrayed,

Conclusion

can be a truly beautiful process of healing and restoration.

Although I wish it were all roses, butterflies, cupcakes, and rainbows, community integration will be a step-by-step process of understanding when to step in and when to withdraw. We must draw boundaries within the context of what is healthy. Withdrawal is a normal and healthy process. Even Jesus withdrew. But we must not call our isolating tendencies withdrawal if it leads to extensive and unhealthy patterns. If we are isolating out of a lens of trauma filters, we may think we are withdrawing when we are isolating. In the context of healthy community in Christian faith, we need to be accountable to come together with those we love and care about, especially when it comes to worship. This is not the same as hanging out, which is also important. Worship and praise are the glue to healthy relationships and community.

One of the final concepts of this book is one of the most important: praise through sudden devastation. When devastation hits, it most definitely will be unexpected. We will then need to turn to prayer and praise in those horrible times. In prison, Paul could have decided that he was going to serve his time, get out of jail, and then find ways to enjoy life through escape. Instead, he turned to praise, and the shackles came off him. The prison doors opened. It was the beginning of his freedom. Paul chose to be transformed by the renewing of his mind in every situation, and we have that same ability today.

We may not have the energy or strength to sing praises in devastating circumstances, but we can choose to embrace this environment and atmosphere. We can choose to orient our heart and press in to his nearness in our brokenness. We can choose to remain accountable. We can choose to reach out for help. We can choose to participate in therapy and inner healing. We can choose to speak the things that are hard to speak for our own healing. We may not have control over what happens to us, but we have a choice as to what we do with it, and therein lies the very power that God gave us, the power of self-control. We can't control our circumstances, but we can choose our attitude. Are we flexible and willing to change or stuck in unhealthy patterns?

The last concept we covered is the power of praise. Good people do recover even if you feel like the person who hurt you continues to succeed. Everyone gives an account, and if we leave vengeance in the hands of the Lord, we can trust him and walk in freedom. We can forgive in a way that sets us free and deepens our level of discernment for situations that we may have fallen for in the past.

YOU DON'T NEED TO DROWN

When you picked up this book, you may have felt as if you were drowning. People who experience traumas can be quite overwhelmed, and the pain and devastation can seem to deteriorate you slowly. But no one is too damaged or too far gone to experience healing. Healing is a process. When I was a younger Christian, I thought that when I finally got my healing, I would never go through another hard time again. I truly believed in the supernatural (and still do but just differently now). Whether or not I see a miracle manifest does not make or break my faith. I didn't fall in love with Jesus on my terms and conditions. I felt the tangible embrace of the Father and knew my life would never be the same. So whenever I struggled after that, I did not let my faith waver. At times, I had questions and felt as if I were barely hanging on to the hem of his garment. But I refused to let go because I know who my Father is. The world will pass away. Everything I experience here outside of supernaturally I cannot take with me when my time on this earth is done and neither can you. We must see circumstances for what they are and separate them from the reality that the faith we carry is Jesus's faith in us. His faith is eternal. We can try to let go of him, but he never lets go of us.

After our son started his victory journey with cancer, others would say that they couldn't imagine what they would do if it happened to their child. (I didn't want them to imagine that, so I was glad to hear it.) But in the midst of those questions, I turned to God with the same concern. "How do I reconcile this with Scripture?" And he gave me the perfect answer in John 16:33. "I have told you all this so that you may have peace in me. Here on earth you will have many trials and sorrows. But take heart, because I have overcome the world."

You see, God never told us that when we become Christians, we would never have any more problems. Instead, he says that the things that happen to us work out for the good of those who love Him and are called according to His purpose (my paraphrase of Romans 8:28).

Jesus straight up told us that while we are living here on earth, we won't only have trials and sorrows, but we will have many of them. And when we have them, we would have a source of comfort: him. In him, we have peace because he has overcome the world.

So long as we are going through hard times and looking for peace in the world, we will never find it. We will only ever find peace in him. I attribute every provision of healing to Jesus. Therapies are wonderful, useful, and effective. I totally believe this and have personally experienced it, which is why I know God has called me to become a therapist myself in the near future. At the same time, therapy can only take you so far. Jesus uses therapy to help people, but Jesus himself heals people. The methods can only take us so far apart from him.

So if you find yourself searching for healing in every other place on this planet apart from Jesus Christ himself, I invite you to enter into relationship with him. He was born of the Virgin Mary, suffered, died, and was buried. On the third day, He rose again. He died as a sacrifice for our sins to restore our access to heavenly adoption as sons and daughters of God. When he died, he took the keys of hell and defeated the grave with his resurrection. Historical records give an account for hundreds of witnesses to his resurrection. This really happened and he really existed (exists) whether you accept Jesus as Lord and Savior of your life. He was crucified, died, buried, and rose again, according to secular historical records. He is the one who holds your healing, and you can run to him today.

If you don't know Jesus personally, I pray that

Conclusion

you encounter him the way I did so many years ago. I was broke with fresh injuries on my arm that communicated the depths of self-hatred and pain I was experiencing. God did not treat me differently from everyone else. He embraced me with a tangible warmth I'll never forget, and no matter what difficulties I go through, the feeling of his embrace is the strongest love I have ever experienced. I pray you experience his tangible embrace as he is with you right now.

You don't need a formula to receive him as it is not in the exact wording of the prayer, but if you are struggling to find the right words, you can ask him to embrace you in this way. You can ask for forgiveness for how you have conformed to the patterns of this world out of your own pain. You can ask him to transform your life by the renewing of your mind. You can proclaim your belief and faith in him and his life-changing power. You can ask him to start a relationship with you day in and day out. You can be steadfast in hearing his voice. If you need help, you can repeat the prayer below, but he knows your heart and what's inside you.

"Jesus, I thank you for dying on the cross for me. I believe you are the Son of God, and I desire you to be the Lord of my life. I repent for the ways I have conformed to the patterns of the world. I ask, Lord, to be transformed by the freedom you offered me when you took our sin at the cross. I choose to renew my mind in your truths and to be dedicated to praising and worshiping you. I can be healed only through you. I commit to walking in relationship with you. I give you my hurt and pain. I give you my hopes and dreams. I trust you with every step of my life. Bad things will happen. But through it, you will be with me, and in you, I have peace. I think you for what you are doing in my life, and I praise you forever. In Jesus's name. Amen."

As I said at the beginning of this section, you don't have to drown anymore. You may have felt like you can't breathe, but I think about a specific picture I've seen floating around on social media, a prophetic picture of Jesus. The picture is angled up at the sky, and Jesus is on the water, reaching for you as you sink. Raise your hands to him and then keep them there. Praise him. Praise when times are good, and

Conclusion

praise through sudden devastation. Praise through the process of healing. Praise when you feel like it and when you don't. This is not your end. This is your new life in Christ. You are his child now. It's only the beginning.

RESOURCE PAGE

On this page, you will find a list of resources if you are in trauma, crisis, or addiction. For some, reaching out to the resources on this page is kind of a big deal. It can feel embarrassing. At times when I went to reach out for help, I worried that people would find out or gossip. What would that do to my reputation? What if people learned that I needed professional counseling for a season because of abuse I endured in ministry? What if people know I went to inner healing? The process can be even more intimidating when it comes to other mental health issues, such as addiction. Addiction hits people of all walks of life, people of every professional and socioeconomic status. While I'd love to tell you that people don't gossip or it won't affect your relationships in any way, I would be lying. Sometimes you might be a victim of those things, but the relationships you are worried about protecting by staying in addiction are not the ones that are the best for you anyway. Break out of the bounds of addiction by first putting aside what anyone may think and going after the help you need. Please note that the following links will also be posted at my website **MillieJoy.com**.

The first resource I highly recommend is Celebrate Recovery which is a Christian-based recovery program: CelebrateRecovery.com

Another option is Alcoholics Anonymous. This is a link to 24-7 online support: https://www.aahomegroup.org

If you are in need of a sexual abuse lawyer, I recommend: Bozlawpa.com

To find a good therapist in your region, I highly recommend going to PsychologyToday.com. On this website, you can put in your location and find mental health professionals in your area with different profiles and payment options. Some work on a sliding scale, and some list that they are Christian-based. Many of you know my journey with inner healing and deliverance ministries and how very careful I am about making referrals. I strongly recommend

Mashah Inner Healing and Deliverance Ministries at MashahMinistry.com. If you schedule a session with this ministry, you can also request that I am on your prayer team. I would love the great honor of doing so.

For crisis mental health help, please call **988**. There, you can instantly access help.

Lastly you can book your live coaching sessions with myself, Millie Joy, at:

WWW.MILLIEJOY.COM

<u>Other Titles by Millie Joy Radosti:</u>
Daddy Issues A New Life
Let's Get Shift Done: Manifesting Your Destiny with a Sound Mind

<u>Titles by Rob Radosti:</u>
And He Unleashed Me to the World
Supernatural Evangelism 101
Happy Holiness: The Rise of Redemptive Reformers
Professor Rob Radosti's Big Bad Doctrine Detox 2.0

ORDER YOUR COPIES AT CHURCH14.COM

Manufactured by Amazon.ca
Acheson, AB

15694615R00142